Responsibility

Becoming the Authentic Man

James Ray & Myles Dhillon

Copyright © 2024
All rights reserved.

ISBN:
9798324627805

Contents

Foreword 5

Introduction 8

Chapter 1 - FIERCE & TENDER 22

Chapter 2 - RIGHT & WRONG 48

Chapter 3 - SORRY & FORGIVING 68

Chapter 4 - CONNECT & ABANDON 91

Chapter 5 - FUN & HEALTHY 113

Chapter 6 - FIRST & LAST 127

Chapter 7 - SONS & FATHERS 146

Conclusion 174

Appendix A, B & C 179

Responsibility

Foreword

Myles and James are always trying to improve. They want to learn, take feedback and grow in every area. Both of them listen and take feedback. I know for Myles, his desire is to be the best he can be. Whether that is as a husband, Dad, in his work or as a friend. Myles decided last year to create a feedback form for every member of our family: my parents, his parents – he even sent it to my dad's executive assistant. He was desperate to get honest feedback so that he could learn and grow. Most of our family members thought he was mad and said we can 'chat next time I see you,' and couldn't take it seriously. Who would really want to be told the worst things about them, straight to their face? The drive to become a better man has always been there. His friendship with James is based on that. They are not perfect, but, luckily, they know that and are open to change.

I have been married to Myles for 13 years; we have three children, and we have lived in different countries. There have been so many different seasons of our married lives. There are many things I love about him. But Myles is not really like anyone I have ever met. When I first met him (before we started dating) I was trying to work out: is he mad or just unique? Did he really want to 'go feed the ducks,' or was he asking me on a date? When he told me he would eat the flowers he gave me to show how much he loved me, he did eat them! He is not trying to be anyone else, not worried what people think about him. His impulsiveness and desire to be different, have adventures and exploit every opportunity, has made sure our life is never dull. Things never stay the same and he is always seeking new challenges, and whatever he puts his mind to, he is all in. He is all in as a husband, as a dad and in the hundreds of new ideas he gets. Whatever he puts his mind to he gives it everything and this I love the most.

Becs Dhillon

*

Finding someone who's truly authentic is rare. But in this book, you'll meet James – my husband – who's the real deal.

We met when we were 12 years old, started dating at 14 and seven years later, we were married. Now, after three decades together, experiencing the highs and lows, it's clear that James doesn't shy away from tough stuff; he prefers to tackle issues head-on, pressing for resolution, and encourages others to do the same. He confronts the shadows of his own experiences, never giving up despite the tough times. I'll admit it, facing up to the hard and painful things isn't always easy, especially with James – it's actually often quite annoying and difficult. But continuously holding up the mirror to each other has resulted in a relationship filled with trust, love, risk, fun, growth and hope.

As you read this book you won't find statistics and charts. Instead you'll be presented with a more empirical-based study; honest, raw insights from real-life experiences from our lives, Becs and Myles' lives and from other men who we've met along the way. I think James is a bit fortunate in this regard; he is instinctively good at connecting – whether it is with our boys, our friends, people on the street or people in the board room, he seems to be able to be himself and to draw out the meaningful things. But I also think that it's not all good fortune; he has been proactive in this, with years of hard work and self-examination. I said he is truly authentic and by that I mean, what you see is actually what you get. He doesn't need to hide anything, he doesn't need to be worried about being exposed, he doesn't need to feel intimidated, because he knows and shows who he is and that's enough. I love that about him. It's inspiring.

This book is written with a passion James and Myles share everywhere they go. I know their hope and desire is to encourage others, without judgment, to reject excuses, overcome limitations and be the best versions of themselves and I really hope you find something of true value within these pages.

Emiko Ray

INTRODUCTION

Whenever you meet someone, it's usual to make introductions. So here's ours.

But first meet Eddy.

Eddy was Myles' grandfather on his mother's side. He grew up in a Welsh mining village. His father was a miner, and Eddy himself would also work in the mines, riding the trolley-lift hundreds of feet underground to chip away at the coal-face for pittance. When the Second World War broke out, Eddy served his country, fighting overseas. Afterwards he moved to west London and trained as an engineer, then set up his own company which he eventually sold.

Eddy married Myles' grandma Mary, and they had three children, then nine grandchildren. Myles knew his grandad as a man who would cry openly, who loved his grandkids with great affection. He was a patient and deeply moral man who always had time for Myles, no matter what. Eddy could accept when he was in the wrong, when he shouldn't have lost his temper, and was always ready to say sorry when that was the right thing to do, often with tears in his eyes. He accepted Myles' father Sid (a first generation immigrant from India) into his family when cross-cultural marriages were a rarity. Eddy came to love Sid and always treated him like his own son. Sid called him 'Dad'. Eddy was always open to learning more, always interested in the wider world and in his grandson's life. Eddy was giving and generous.

In Myles' mind, his grandad was the complete package: the consummate example of how to be a man.

Introduction

Perhaps above all, Eddy and Mary modelled the most stunning vision of marriage – even when Eddy was lying on his deathbed, his face distorted, saliva frothing at the corners of his mouth, unable to communicate with nothing more than groans. When visiting hours were over, Mary would climb onto Eddy's hospital bed for a good night cuddle, and kiss him on the lips, froth and all. Myles remembers his grandad still mustering the energy to slide his hand down Mary's back for a cheeky pat on her bum. Eddy loved Mary to the very end. For Myles, their life was an inspiring vision of how good a marriage could truly be.

Except recently, Myles' adoring image of his late grandad was shattered in a single moment. He happened to be talking with his mother about Eddy when she casually dropped into conversation, 'Oh yes, that was around the time Dad was having an affair with ▇▇▇.' (Name hidden for identity privacy) BAM!

The words hit Myles like a sucker punch to the gut. At first he was sure he must have heard her wrong. He steadied himself against the kitchen counter. He felt sick. His eyes filled with tears. The breath caught in his throat.

▇▇▇ was someone Mary knew well. In one shocking moment Myles felt his world fall apart. For weeks afterwards, he couldn't even talk about it. Even when his mother tried to explain what had happened, he just couldn't go there. It was too painful.

For Myles, Eddy had been the model of integrity, of decency, of all that was good and right in the world. He had been the template of manhood which Myles hoped to emulate for the rest of his life. When that image was smashed like a broken mirror, Myles was left reeling. After all, what do you look to when you discover all you believed was best and truest in the world is a lie?

*

The *In-Authentic* Man
This story is almost the perfect embodiment of what we want this book to address. The problem of the inauthentic man. The man who looks like he lives one way but actually is living another.

Now you may think that Myles was over-reacting. The same kind of revelation might not provoke such an extreme response in you as it did in Myles. After all, we're all human, aren't we? We all make mistakes. The trouble was Myles had elevated his grandfather onto such a high pedestal. Eddy was a hero to him, a role model, so for Myles, one stumble was all it took to completely disillusion him, throwing into question how he was supposed to stand up and be a man.

This book hopes to speak into that problem.

*

The Two Problems Men Face
We think there are two main problems in our current society that relate to masculinity.

The first is a more recent development, a topic of discussion that seems to be widespread in our day: the idea that masculinity itself is in crisis. Often it's been suggested that one of the great blights on Western society is 'toxic masculinity' – a term that is supposed to encapsulate a certain type of behaviour in men.

But Eddy's story actually speaks more directly into the second problem, which for us is more real and pressing: that men are inauthentic and don't live out their true potential. They don't know who they really are; consequently they don't live out of that self-knowledge to become the best men they could be. This book attempts to address these two problems *together* and the solution we want to present to both of them is what we call the **Authentic Man.**

We want to invite men into a journey to become the Authentic Man.

So who or what is the Authentic Man?

The fuller answer to that question is what this book is all about. But to at least introduce the concept, we think it's helpful first to explain what the Authentic Man is not.

Being 'authentic' in the way we wish to use the word does not mean how it has sometimes been used elsewhere: the idea that this is me, and only I get to say exactly what that looks like. You just have to accept me as I am, including what I want to do and say, whether you like it or not. And that is me being authentic.

No. Authenticity as a kind of supercharged form of self-expression is not what we are talking about. Our definition of 'authentic' is more about integrity. It's about being the opposite of inauthentic in the

sense of not being a fake – of presenting one thing, but in fact being quite another. Being authentic to us means being the same on the outside as you are on the inside.

Someone who's external image, reputation and appearance matches the life he is actually living behind closed doors.

But this kind of authenticity is more than just knowing who you are and what you want and then presenting that to the world. We think that the authentic 'you' should be challenged and mediated (and changed) by the needs and expectations of the wider world around you – of partners, family, community, and culture – and also by what is ultimately healthier and better for you.

Thus, the Authentic Man is a kind of ideal towards which we want to point you. In that sense, following (or even pursuing) the Authentic Man is about discovering truth. The truth of who you are but more importantly the truth of what you could become. Looking ahead at the Authentic Man and seeing what you could be. Perhaps what you should be.

Sometimes the Authentic Man might be visible out there in front of us in someone else. Sometimes others might be able to glimpse the Authentic Man in us. But for all men, the Authentic Man represents this true ideal. A true guide, if you like, who can lead us beyond the pitfalls and mires into which we all have a tendency to fall, towards firmer, higher ground.

Better ground. For us and for everyone around us.

It might feel as though we are presenting this as a kind of cookie-cutter form of masculinity – a template to which men should conform. But in fact, the genius of the Authentic Man is quite different. He is not a carbon copy template of what manhood is or should be. But rather he offers a direction of travel – more like a true north. And we hope that by following him, men will journey into the fullness of who they could be, discovering and realising the fullness of their own gifts and personality and individuality, a process which will draw out of each man his individual flavours and colours in all of their richness and glory.

So we can all learn from others what it is to be the Authentic Man. And we can all model to others the Authentic Man. Yet he remains an ideal to journey towards. A destination we never quite reach, but which encourages us to travel far.

The journey to becoming the Authentic Man is a life-long quest to find the true self, and then to live it out. It's not only about who I want to be, it's about who I am compelled to be, who I am called to be. Who I am expected to be. As a man. Because masculinity also fits into the wider community. On the whole, what is good for you as an individual should also be good for your family, for your community, for the wider world.

So how do we hold those these seemingly opposing ideas of self and others together?

*

Balance
Often men end up in extremes. For any given set of characteristics you're either at this end of a spectrum or at that one. For example, we are either rich or poor; fit or unfit; old or young; fierce or

tender; strong or weak. The problem with these dualisms is that too easily they can become binary and simplistic, both in the way we see ourselves and the way others see us. Think about it: you are not either rich or poor, fit or unfit, old or young, because in each category there are gradations of wealth, fitness, age etc. You may be poorer than those people, but you are certainly richer than these others. You might wish you were younger, but you are glad you are not so old that...etc...and so it goes on.

What we have tried to do in this book is unpack some of these apparently binary extremes and show that the reality is often more grey than black and white. We look for that middle ground and say perhaps you could be both. Perhaps there are times when you really should be both.

We have chosen the different chapters in this book in order to address the **balance** we need in our life as men – the balance of a man holding himself in the tension of both. Each chapter sets out how to find the balance between certain attributes which we think the Authentic Man will cultivate in his life. It is by no means an exhaustive list. We haven't the time or space to explore an entirely comprehensive survey of the male human experience. In any case, you will have your own challenge to find the right balance in your life. But we hope the areas we discuss will prove helpful to setting you on the right path.

Remember: the Authentic Man is the ideal of every man, of any man. And because it is an ideal, as we said, it represents a destination that can never be reached. You'll never be able to declare, *'That's it. I've made it. I am now the Authentic Man,'* anymore than by heading west, you'll be able to catch the sunset. Like the movement of the sun, it is a new experience every day. Every day there is more to consider. More to change. More to do. As an ideal, it will always be beyond you, just out of reach. But that shouldn't put you off, or stop you from trying.

It's the direction of travel, towards something better, that makes the journey worth the taking.

*

Why Us?
Anyone who writes a book will be familiar with the feeling of impostor syndrome. After all, it's a very real and legitimate question: why would we – James Ray and Myles Dhillon – decide that we needed to write a book on masculinity, other than the fact we happen to be two men? We've wrestled with this question for some time. And the reason is certainly not that we think we have all the answers to the challenges of being a man. In fact, the opposite is closer to the truth. This journey towards becoming the Authentic Man is our own journey. Something we are on together.

All the same, we have had some experience which, we think, has given us something to say.

Several years ago, we signed up for a trip to Belgium where we went on an expedition with a group of Dutch men. There, we were inspired by the idea that leading men out into the wild on a big outdoor adventure creates a space for them to be more open about the adventures and the struggles that they are having on the inside. The outdoors creates an environment for them to be real, raw and honest. Impressed by the impact the expedition had had on us and on the other men in the group, we accepted the challenge to bring back this model – internationally called The 4M Movement – to the UK and set up something similar.

Since then, we have taken thousands of men away into the wilderness on what we call 'Xtreme Character Challenges' or 'XCC's.' These long weekends represent mind-body-soul adventures for men, events where men are challenged physically, mentally, relationally, spiritually and emotionally. Sort of like an MOT for blokes, a check-up in all areas of your life.

This experience has effectively given us thousands of 'clinical' hours walking with thousands of men on their journeys and ours, discussing the very things of life that we will highlight in this book. We have heard countless men's stories about the good, the bad, and the ugly in their lives. Whilst we don't quote these stories directly – they are not our stories to share and that could be a whole other book – the evidence which underpins the thinking of much of this book is drawn from the thousands of stories we've heard and conversations we've had.

To give you some idea, on just one of these long weekends, we have more hours of conversation with other men about the deeper issues of life (which they would rarely talk about elsewhere) than many do with their regular friends for the entire rest of the year. In fact, often in a single weekend guys cover more ground with a total stranger than most blokes would with some of their closest friends in the course of a lifetime. And it's from these conversations that certain themes reveal themselves. Themes that are so consistent across cultures, across ages, across demographics, that they start to feel like universal struggles and challenges which all men are going through in our current times.

After some years of this, we have started to appreciate the value of everything we have been privileged enough to hear, and recognise the unique position we are in to identify some of the pitfalls into which men are prone to fall time and again. More positively, we've also begun to formulate some strategies and solutions that can help men climb out of and continue onward from those pitfalls if they do.

*

Who Are We?
We want this book to be almost like a conversation between the two of us and you. Therefore, it may be helpful to know a little more about who we are.

James has come at this book with more of a thinking mindset, natural enough given his background in training and cognitive theory, teaching and coaching. He has been speaking about masculinity in the public sphere for some years now, mostly at conferences, on podcasts and TV shows. He continues to run the Xtreme Character Challenge movement in the UK. Besides this, he is a leadership consultant, he used to be a private school house master, and he was in the Royal Navy reserves for a time. He is married to his childhood sweetheart Emiko and they have two boys and an adoptive son. This is the lens through which James sees masculinity.

Myles, on the other hand, has a different background and a different approach, which is more about the illustration and application of the ideas. Myles has an uncanny ability to illustrate an abstract theory through a simple story, often based on his own life experience. Myles started out his career in music. But he has progressed from rapping through property development into plumbing. He's worked for charities and NGOs, he's run his own businesses, he's invested in bitcoin, he's set up start-up companies in India. He grew up in Maidenhead, but if you met him, you might think he'd sprung from the gang culture of inner city London. Myles is married to Becs and has three children.

Myles has a white British mother and an Indian father. James has white blond hair, looks like a Viking and has a plummy accent. You'd think he went to private school (even though he didn't). Myles is brown and acts like he's a bit gee'd up. But for all of our differences, we are actually not dissimilar, especially in our outlook on what it means to be a man.

Whilst we come from very different starting points in life – and often people who see us together can't quite figure out how we are such good friends – we have ended up holding very similar views. We can usually anticipate the other's reaction to any given problem. Ultimately that has been the foundation of our friendship. At times, we've worried that writing this book would be the ruin of all that we shared. There were moments when it came close. But in the end we actually think it has reset our friendship on even firmer footing.

The reality is we are just two blokes, sharing what wisdom we've gleaned from our own experience and that of thousands of other men. And also from our own pain, our own challenges, our own mistakes, our own failures.

To discover what that looks like, read on.

*

Why Do We Want Men To Succeed?
Even as we write these words, James is looking at a tattoo on Myles' right arm which says 'Passion'. Passion is the name of one of his kids, but it is also something that unites us both, especially on certain topics. We are passionate about understanding what goes wrong with men, and what can be done to set them on a better path. We are passionate to see men succeed in this area for two fundamental reasons.

First, we both share a deep belief that, as men, our role on this earth matters. As a friend, a husband, a father, a brother, a son – it is crucial that our role be played out well.

Second, we need each other. Men need other positive and healthy men in their lives. In our case, this has come quite naturally. Despite some poor role models in our families, neither of us feel that threatened by other men. We are fortunate to feel quite comfortable in our own spheres and our place within them. We don't see ourselves in competition with other men. Both of us have had quite unusual life journeys, experiencing lots of change and diverse influences. This has made us both open and adaptable; we are as comfortable with the poorest of the poor as the richest of the rich (as you'll see from some of our stories). What unites us and informs our friendship is a desire to be better men. So we think why not take others along with us on the journey towards that goal?

That's what we hope to achieve with this book. To

gather other men together to go on a journey with us. For us, this book is an open invitation, from us to you. An invitation to come with us and discover for yourself, not to sit at our feet and learn. Rather let's walk together, side by side.

The XCC weekends are all about walking side by side with other men. So often we have listened to their stories, seen their brokenness, and felt saddened by it. It's inspired in us a desire to help men live out better stories. And no man's story is over while there's still breath in his body. There is still time. However bad it has been up to this point, it's possible for every one of us to live out the rest of our story better.

It's important that we do. Because living out a better story isn't just better for men. It's better for women, for children, for our communities. For our world.

We don't offer single simplistic answers. We prefer to ask questions, often challenging questions. But we are confident you will find the answers to those questions for yourself. We want you to be the hero of your own story. We want you to become the best version of who you can be. Because, let's face it – if you can be that, then so can we. We are all connected to each other. We're in this together.

So we invite you on an adventure now. The adventure of becoming the Authentic Man.

*

Use this book however you want. You might want to read it chapter by chapter. Or cover to cover in one sitting (it's not too long). Or you might want to mix up the chapters as the mood takes you. Each one should stand on its own. You might also want to make notes in the margin.

Chapter One

FIERCE & TENDER

We live in a physical world. Matter matters. What we see is what we can trust. Seeing is believing.

Physical traits are an important indicator of the essence of a thing. Elephants are big. Mice are small. The grass is green. The sea is wet. That is a core part of what they are.

So what is true for the world around us is also true for us as human beings. Men and women each have their own physicality. It says something about them. Equal but different. In this chapter, we want to look at this difference more closely.

*

Physicality
Most of us can tell most men from most women just by looking at them. Most men have a recognisable physical appearance that distinguishes them from most women. Men are proportionally bigger than women. This seems to be a basic fact of the human species.

Throughout ancient history, men's physical strength has often been put to use in jobs that suit the bulkier of the two sexes. An obvious example is combat in warfare, for the most part carried out by men. But there are many others.

It's men whom we sent down the coal mines. It's men who built our towns and our cities. It's men who worked the land, who sailed the seas.

In more recent decades, however, things have changed dramatically. New developments in the division of labour across Western society – first through industrialisation, then automation and now digitalisation – have meant that men's physical strength relative to women has lost much of its more obvious value. It makes no difference how strong you are when you're sitting in front of a computer screen. These changes have opened up new opportunities for women, enabling the gap between the sexes to close.

All this is very good. And yet, the physical differences between men and women remain.

So what are we to make of them?

When it comes to our physicality, there seem to be two ways for men to go wrong. At one extreme, you have men who are violent, overly aggressive, wild, out of control. A danger and a menace to everyone around them. At the other, you find men who are too soft, too passive, too weak. Men who take no responsibility, who are too willing to drift with whatever comes along next.

The two words we will use that characterise these two extremes are **fierce** and **tender**.

The trend of recent years has been to push men in one direction: towards being more tender. The more traditional markers of being a bloke – tough, strong, capable, courageous – have been tainted as being potentially toxic. The fear is that too often those traits spill into excessive aggression, domination and violence, especially towards women. Instead, men have been expected to cultivate their gentle side, their creativity, being in touch with their feelings.

But the one-sided nature of all this has created a kind of vacuum for men – for young men, in particular, who are trying to figure out what sort of man they should become as they move forward into adulthood. Being soft and kind and tender is of great value and much needed in today's society, but without also addressing the reality of the fierce end of the spectrum of masculinity, it feels to many men that something is missing.

Wherever there's a vacuum, nature fills it, and it's been too easy for this one to be filled with the wrong voices. The wrong answers.

Right now, masculinity feels like a battlefield in fog. Men are confused. On one hand, the media and public commentators seem very clear about what they think is 'toxic masculinity'. On the other, there is little cultural consensus about what *healthy* masculinity actually looks like. Meanwhile men are crying out for some wisdom and guidance to move forward through the fog. Not least on this important issue: how to strike the right balance between being fierce and being tender.

That is exactly what we're going to explore in this chapter.

*

Fierce and Tender - Two Stories
James used to teach at a school in Switzerland. One of the school nurses was young and active: she loved skiing, she loved the outdoors, she was popular. Her boyfriend was a ski guide. One day, on a day-off, they decided to go backcountry skiing, trekking way off piste where no one else goes. They ended up in an area on the back of the biggest

mountain in the Alps, Mont Blanc. They were having a great day together. At a certain point, they skied into an area where the risk of avalanche could sometimes be high. But since there hadn't been any snow for a while, they felt they were safe enough to continue across.

Unfortunately, sometimes the wild can surprise you. Accidents happen. And while they were crossing that area, something triggered an avalanche above them. All of a sudden the snow came pouring down the mountain towards them like a tidal wave. Watching an avalanche from a distance, it's easy to think, 'Oh, I'll just out-ski that.' But in reality, the mass of snow tears down the slope with deceptive and increasing speed and power. It's almost impossible to get out of its way once it's coming right at you. And it's not just soft fluffy powder coming at you. It's rocks and boulders and large lumps of ice ripping down the mountain. (Imagine chimney stacks flying at your head.) Within seconds, you are engulfed. And this is what happened to the school nurse and her boyfriend. They were caught directly in the avalanche's path. In an instant they were buried.

When that happens, often you die not because you're suffocated, but because you're crushed by these big blocks of ice.

Eventually, the couple were declared missing and the authorities launched a rescue party at once. They tracked the couple's route and made their way up into the affected area to try to find any trace of them. It is hard work, digging and searching through blocks of ice and packed snow. Finally they found them, buried under the churned up terrain among the lumps of rock and ice. They were dead, their bodies entombed in the snow. But the remarkable thing was that the body of the boyfriend was shielding the body of the nurse. He had cocooned her inside his arms. He was wrapped around and over her with his back to the uphill slope against the brunt of the avalanche's onslaught. Though they were both killed, the way in which the ski guide had done his best to physically shield the nurse made such an impression on those who found them that their tragic story became a local legend almost immediately.

When James first heard the story, he thought, 'What a guy. Yes, it was a terrible tragedy – but what a guy!' That in those awful last moments, the guide had chosen to throw himself over his girlfriend in the vain hope that she might survive. Out of pure instinct, he had chosen to use all of his size, all of his physicality, to stop what proved the unstoppable force of the avalanche. That was truly heroic. He was known as a sweet and gentle guy. But in that moment, he was fierce. When the avalanche was coming, he was ready to throw his body in its path to protect her. And by the way, it wasn't as if the nurse was a weak and incapable person herself. She was a very strong, capable and independent woman.

At the same time as being fierce, he was tender. His action was to protect her. And although they both died, in those last moments, she knew that she was as cared for and protected as she could possibly have been in that situation. And he knew clearly where his passion and purpose should be directed. That is real tenderness. You could almost say a fierce tenderness.

Could we ever hope to act the same?

Contrast this with another story we heard. A newlywed couple went on honeymoon to South Africa. One evening as they were walking back to their hotel, they were held up by a gang of armed robbers. The gang leader quickly took most of their valuables off them. But when it came to stealing their solid gold wedding rings, he couldn't get either one off their fingers. Not wanting to miss out on more profit, he told the couple that the robbery was hardly worth the trouble if he didn't take at least one of the rings. For this he needed to cut off a finger - he didn't care which one. After that they could go free. Whose finger was their choice to make. But, he warned, if both refused, then he would kill them. So who was it to be? The man or his wife?

At first the man stepped forward and held out his trembling hand. But as the robber seized his wrist and got ready to cut, the man's nerve failed and at the last moment he snatched back his hand, saying he couldn't do it. The robbers became angry now, one of them telling the leader that they should just kill them both and be done with it. So the wife, seeing they were deadly serious about carrying out their threat, stepped forward in her husband's place. This time her nerve held. And within moments, the robbers had severed her finger and made off with her ring and the rest of their valuables, leaving the couple on the street. Of course, they were relieved to be alive, but they also knew that now everything between them had changed. It's no surprise that the marriage failed soon afterwards.

How could it survive once the woman knew that, when it really counted, her husband wouldn't stand up for her? He wasn't fierce enough to defend her. It didn't matter how tender or loving he was when all was well. When the threat came, when she needed

Responsibility

him the most, he had shown that he wasn't prepared to take the hit for her. He literally wouldn't put his body on the line.

Now, before anyone thinks we are trying to present some sort of old fashioned etiquette of manners – something like men always holding doors open for women – or in this case, that the man should always step in to protect the woman – just pause for a second...we think it's deeper than that.

Imagine for a second if the positions in each story were reversed. Imagine if, after the avalanche, it was the nurse found protecting her ski guide boyfriend. How does that picture make you feel? It's not the same, is it? Doesn't it feel off somehow? It doesn't matter how strong or independent the woman may be. That's beside the point. We think there is something natural about the positioning of the man and the woman that way round, not because of the genders involved, but because it was the physically stronger person protecting the weaker. The 'weaker' could be a woman, could be another man, could be a child. Could even be an animal. But their positioning feels the right way round. And so far, everyone we've spoken to about this story has agreed. We're not suggesting this as hard evidence, it's more a feeling, a sense of things. An innate understanding of the way things should be.

In the same way, if the newlywed husband had held his nerve and sacrificed his finger to save both their lives, that may feel dramatic but somehow it feels like the way it should be. He would have done what was necessary to protect his wife. But in the moment, he couldn't. Or he didn't.

Both men's responses were instinctive. Decisions

taken in the moment. And you might think, well, if our response is instinctive, what can I do about it? It's an uncontrolled reaction. I'll only discover if I have what it takes in that moment.

No.

We want to challenge that way of thinking. It's too passive. Because we can take action before the danger comes. We can train our instincts now so that when the 'avalanche' hits, we act like the ski guide and not the shrinking husband.

We both want our response to be that way round.

When we first started thinking about this, we kept coming back to the idea that, as men, we need to be ready.

Most of the time we should be tender and gentle and kind. But when the call comes, we need to be able and ready to fight.

We hope most of us would recognise what we mean by this. At some point or other, we've been that guy walking home alone at night in some town or city. It's late, the streets are close to deserted. Even with headphones on and a hood pulled up, we become hyper-aware of ourselves and our surroundings. We know exactly where our phone is, our wallet is. We sense and keep track of every person in our periphery. We are in a state of heightened anticipation: that *if* someone were to come at us, we are ready to defend ourselves. We might even play out different scenarios in our head and how we should respond.

Ready to run; or ready to fight. *If necessary.*

For some, being ready might mean something a little different.

A few years ago, Myles and his wife, Becs, were preparing to move to India. Knowing India was a very different culture to their own, where personal safety in public is less guaranteed, Myles wanted to be sure that he would be able to handle himself if something bad were to happen. So he joined a boxing gym and started learning how to fight. He was reasonably fit and strong already, but he wanted to be sure that, if it came down to it, he could throw a punch. And more importantly that he could take one.

Professor Scott Atkinson in his 2017 article in the *Guardian* newspaper, 'Why men fight - and what it says about masculinity' explores the idea of what it is in men that makes them instinctively want to fight. And perhaps more significantly, how they often play out in their heads *how* they might handle themselves in a fight if it came down to it. As Atkinson says, 'We may know that fighting is dumb, but we still have the instinctive desire to do it.'

Often the way a fight plays out in our imaginations is neat and heroic. Usually the reality is anything but. Most of the time it's scrappy, confusing, disjointed, inconclusive, shockingly painful and ultimately dissatisfying.

Even so, when thinking about the need to be fierce, we understood it as something needed in the moment. When someone breaks into our home, or when someone threatens our family or a child or an elderly person – someone else in need of protection. Something to be deployed maybe 1% of the time; while the other 99%, a man should be tender, kind and gentle.

But eventually our thinking evolved. We decided the idea that fierceness is something that we might need only once in a blue moon isn't quite right. The split between the two started to feel artificial. Instead we realised what was needed was for *both* dials to be turned all the way up, all of the time.

Always tender. Always fierce.

*

Fire is Always Fire
To be always tender and always fierce probably sounds like a contradiction, and you may well be wondering what that looks like.

To help with this, let's consider the analogy of fire.

Whether in the form of a little candle-flame on top of a birthday cake, or a raging wildfire threatening to destroy a whole town, fire always has essentially the same nature. Fire is always itself. It doesn't change.

Fire can be both fierce and tender. How it's handled determines which it's going to be.

Think about it. Most fires going on around us, most days, are put to positive, creative uses. Consider the ways we use fire around our homes. Fire warms us, cooks for us, helps us stay clean. Fire powers our vehicles. Fire has taken us to the Moon. Fire lights our cigarettes. Harnessing the power of fire is arguably man's greatest innovation. But fire must always be handled with care because its nature is always the same. It's always hot, always edgy, potentially dangerous. You don't muck about with fire.

But fire can also be tender. Think about how comforting it is to warm yourself by a fire when you're cold. Or the romantic glow of a candle-lit room. Or a beacon signal to guide you home.

The same is true with our idea of masculinity. Men should always be ready to defend someone or something, when that's the right thing to do. That is fierce. But it's a fierceness under control. Like the flame inside your boiler.

The risk is, if we think about our fierceness only as something to unleash once a year, that we'll only associate this fierceness with physical violence. We suggest fierceness is more like fire – quietly burning away among the coals most of the time – mostly to heat things, to help with things, to get things done. To our minds, this is a much more useful way of framing what drives our masculinity.

In other words, our fierceness becomes the furnace within us that powers everything in our lives.

How and when to turn it up and let it roar is what we'll look at now.

*

Wrong Time, Wrong Place
Myles' Dad, Sid, has no problem with being fierce. He's ready whenever and wherever to let his fierce side off the leash. And as a younger man, Sid was quite a fighter. One childhood memory that's hard for Myles to forget is when his family were queuing in heavy traffic to get onto a ferry. There was a motorist dodging and weaving between the

different lanes of traffic to work his way up the queue. Sid took exception to this. He got out of the car and walked forward past the other cars to confront the queue-jumper. Sun blazing in the height of summer, the argument soon got heated. The other man took a swipe at Sid through his open window, but being restrained by his seatbelt, the blow didn't land. Instead, Sid shoved him back inside the car, then leaned in and snatched the keys from the ignition. The man looked on in horror as he dropped the keys down a nearby drain. Sid then returned to the car to the ringing cheers of the other motorists in the queue – at least that's the way he remembers it!

Another time, only a few weeks back, he was helping Myles remove an old boiler from a house he was working on, before installing a new one. While the clapped out boiler was sat on the pavement, a local resident came up and started pulling off the copper piping around the bottom. This was annoying, mainly because Myles had arranged for a scrap metal merchant to collect the boiler, but if all the valuable copper had been stripped, the merchant wouldn't take it and Myles would have to do an extra trip to the dump. When Myles confronted the local, telling him it wasn't his to take, the man told Myles he was going to have it anyway, and what was he going to do about it. At that point, Sid walked out of the house and a full-blown row ensued. Sid got so wound up that he threatened to put the boiler through the man's van window after he had made some adjustments to his nose. The local replied that he'd chuck it straight back through Myles' windscreen if he did. All of this for a few quids' worth of copper.

(Eventually Sid backed off and the guy made off

with his copper, unchallenged.)

Clearly there's a question of proportion when it comes to how we respond to a threat. Being hyper-sensitive to a threat or any kind of offence may seem like a good way to be ready, but ultimately it's likely to cause more problems than it solves. We don't want a hair-trigger temper, putting us so on edge that we kick off at the slightest provocation.

But more important than the question of *when* is the question of *what* we are defending.

To be clear, we're talking about being fierce protectors, not aggressors. The last thing we're advocating is unprovoked aggression. But even if our fierceness is defensive, if all we're defending is me and what's mine – my tribe, my clan, myself, my ego, my stuff – then it has limited value. Think of the ski guide again. If he was found curled in a ball protecting himself, we'd hardly think he was heroic.

*

The Guard & The Gardener
So how do we know what we should fight for? It's a problem as old as mankind itself: if man is a fighter, which battles should he fight? Having the wisdom and discernment to figure this out is one of the main aims of this book.

So far, we've only really talked about physical things.

The physicality of men, standing up, ready to fight. But we want to broaden our thinking now to include anything against which we might struggle. Not just physical assailants in a dark alley or intruders in the home, but the non-physical assailants that surround us. The assaults on our minds, on our relationships, on our finances, on the vulnerable and the powerless around us. On our values – the things we think are good and true and right.

When we start thinking along those lines, we realise why we need to be always on. Because we live in a state of constant war. We live in a power-hungry, money-grabbing, ideologically aggressive world. We live in a world that often wants to take the things we have. To damage or disregard the things that are precious to us. So we need to be protective. This protection may look very different from one situation to the next, but the goal is the same: to keep safe what we value in order that it may flourish.

With this in mind, we have found the image of a **home** helpful. Imagine a simple home: there's a house, a little surrounding land, a garden, all of it enclosed by a protective wall or a fence. This home represents and contains all that you hold precious, all that you value, including your partner, your family and the things you love. But it also represents your values, your sense of justice, your sense of what is right and wrong. The fence represents your boundaries.

We want everything inside the home to flourish and grow. We want to protect everything within the outer wall from any destructive forces and threats that come in from the outside. In this sense, there are two roles for us, as men, to play. These align with our ideas of fierce and tender.

One role is the **guard**, the fierce protector with one eye on the perimeter. The guard is a warrior. The guard is fierce and strong and able to fight. But for everything inside the wall, the other role is the **gardener**. This role is tender and creative and gentle – a gardener, a builder, an artist, a father, a husband, a lover, a friend.

As a man, you have to learn the context in which you are to focus on one role or the other. But to be the Authentic Man, you need to be aware that you are both. And you need to cultivate your ability to be both.

Take for example, domestic violence. This sort of fierce and violent outburst within the home is a terrible confusion of these roles. Too much fierceness inside your own boundary is destructive. You are doing your enemy's work for them, destroying and damaging all that you value most and want to protect. That's crazy. It's totally stupid to turn the place that's supposed to be the safest for those dependent on you into a battlefield. It's the exact opposite of what you should be doing, which is nurturing them, tending the garden.

And yet by the same measure, if all you are is a nurturer, then you are neglecting your responsibility to fully safeguard whatever you value. It's no good to put your energy into building and cultivating and loving and nurturing whatever lies within your walls if you leave the gate wide open for anyone to come in and trample over or steal what you love.

It's worth noting that most likely each of us will have a natural weighting in one direction or another. It's just part of our make-up; we're born that way. Some of us are natural guards, and so we probably need more encouragement and practice in being more tender. Others of us are natural gardeners and need practice being fierce. But to be the Authentic Man, the better you need to be at both roles, becoming practised at shifting emphasis between one and the other.

*

Nature Knows
The concept of the Alpha male is one that is often referenced. Yet it is also often misrepresented and largely misunderstood. Young men who think of themselves as Alpha males because they drink a lot of beer and make a lot of noise and get into fights are – apart from being very annoying and tiresome – invariably also very far from being 'alpha' in the strictly sociological sense.

Thanks mainly to its simplistic portrayal in popular culture, most of us carry around a caricature understanding of what Alpha males are really like. This is not the understanding of primatologist Frans De Waal. Through studying chimpanzees, he has revealed that the males who are physically most imposing, violent and aggressive may dominate for a while, but usually not for very long. Eventually, rebelling against his tyrannical rule, the other chimps join forces to overthrow him. Remarkably the male they often replace him with is one who has consistently shown high social skills and connection, kindness and generosity especially with food, and a general skill in mobilising collaboration within the troop. De Waal concludes that this is the true Alpha male.

Think about that for a second.

That is a completely different understanding of the term Alpha male than the one most of us carry around in our heads.

This potentially changes everything. The Alpha male

is not the big, domineering, strong and violent one who comes to a violent end. It's the one who can build peaceful communities, for the benefit of everyone as well as himself. So now we can see ourselves as being an Alpha male when we're being a faithful husband, a dutiful and loving father, a loyal and attentive friend, a defender of the weak – whatever it might be.

That is 'Alpha'. That is a winning strategy.

*

Practise Being Fierce
Remember we said that the two different responses – of the ski guide and then of the husband – were based on instinct. They reacted in the moment. But the groundwork that determined their instinctive response in that moment was laid over a long period leading up to it. As men, we should take a proactive approach to make sure we lay the groundwork in the right way. Practice makes perfect. That goes for both the roles we've been discussing: guard and gardener.

Boxer Mike Tyson famously said, 'Everyone has a plan until they get punched in the mouth.'

Life has many ways of punching us in the mouth. What is our response going to be when it does?

Modern living offers a number of ways that give the appearance of developing our fierce side as men.

Violent video-games, MMA YouTube clips, aggressive chants on the football terrace. Doling out abuse on social media platforms, watching people fighting on TV shows, road raging threats at other drivers from the safety of our locked car doors. These might have the appearance of a kind of toughness, but really they teach us nothing useful.

Or worse, they desensitise us to violence, and are more likely to leave us spectators on the side-line of a battle worth fighting, when really we should be in the thick of it, being fierce protectors, taking the hits.

Hiding in a virtual world of anonymity isn't going to help us. Taking personal responsibility is an important part of stepping up.

So we suggest if you want to make progress in this area, step away from the screens. They'll teach you nothing about this.

Instead, as we said at the start of the chapter, cultivate the physical side of your masculinity. If you happen to have a lot of untapped aggression, join a boxing gym, a martial arts group or a rugby team. Find an outlet where you can harness your physicality and aggression in a positive way.

Go outside. Get uncomfortable. Swim in cold water. Climb a mountain. Challenge yourself. Travel to the limits of who you think you are, and then push those limits a little further.

All of this will hone your fierceness.

But then learn how to apply it. You can become more skilful with practice. There are different degrees. Otherwise it can be a bit like carrying around a golf bag with only a putter and a driver. If that's all you've got in the bag, for any given shot you might smash it too hard or tap it too gently. But if your bag has the full collection of clubs, you can learn to go up through the different levels, depending on what shot you need to make. You can learn to play better. When Myles' Dad threatened that bloke nicking the copper with putting a boiler through his window...that was the wrong club, don't you think? If your wife is shouting at you, ask yourself: which is the right club to play here? Do I yell back at her? No. Channel your fierceness and learn to offer a different response.

All of this is a lot easier said than done. That's why we need practice.

*

Practise Being Tender
Recently, Myles was on a plumbing job fixing up a block of flats. He was working alongside another tradesman whose job it was to abseil down the outside of the building and connect the flue. During a tea break, Myles asked him what it meant to him as a man to be tender. For a minute, he looked at Myles like he'd gone funny in the head. (It's not the sort of question you hear much on a building site.) But once he realised Myles was serious, he thought about it and then said, 'Yeah, I suppose it's good to be nice sometimes. Like when I give the dog a good rub and stroke now and then. That's being tender, isn't it?'

He's not wrong. It is tender. How we interact with animals is often a good sign of how a man will interact with people. But it's also a great way of practising tenderness. If you can look after a dog, if you can be kind to a dog, then you can roll that skill into being kind and tender with humans, too.

One of the toughest people James knows is a builder called Dave. He is a massive man of few words who is capable of being quite brutal with people around him. But James knows that he is still a kind man because he's seen Dave with his own dogs and with James'. This is a guy who will barely speak five words to you, who has struggled with his own mental well-being for years and can't really open up. But he's happy to roll around on the floor with his dogs and give them half his lunch.

So this is something we want to draw out of ourselves as much as possible. Tenderness comes to some of us more naturally than others. But we can all take it just a bit further.

All of us are different. We may find it easier to be affectionate and tender with certain creatures more than others. Men/women; kids/adults; animals/humans. Even plants are better than nothing. The point is we can all start somewhere, and then roll that practised tenderness into other areas of our life.

Start with animals if you like. Start with the person behind the counter serving you a coffee. Start with the guy at work who is on his own. Start with your kids at bedtime. Wherever you start, make a practice of it, and then expand it into the relationships around you that really matter to you.

*

The Enemy Within
Let's shift the thinking for a second. When we think about being fierce, it's easy to think about that in the context of a fight. But we now want to re-frame the word 'fight' into 'struggle'. In the context of any struggle, you can always ask yourself: am I the

aggressor or the protector? What am I struggling for? What am I struggling against?

A struggle to protect others or something other than ourselves of value is a fight worth having. We should struggle where there's injustice. We should struggle where there's an invasion of people's space or values by an aggressor. And here's the important point – *even if the struggle is in my mind, an invasion of my mental space.* In other words, something I am doing that jeopardises or damages my values and beliefs, the things I hold precious in life.

Often the 'enemy within' is the one to which we offer absolutely no resistance.

But we need to, because it can be just as devastating as a threat from outside. Many of us are often ready to front up to another bloke in the pub because of the way he looked at our girlfriend. But far less ready to front up to ourselves about how we looked at a woman on another man's arm. Or maybe it's that extra drink; or that website we shouldn't visit; or that bet we should walk away from; or that text we shouldn't send. We can be masters of undermining our own lives, just as we can be masters of self-deception. Porn, for example, is a real enemy to yourself. It's a serious assault on your mind and body that is going to have an effect on the way you relate to your partner. In your sex life, most obviously – but in other ways too. It can seem so harmless, but so quickly become so harmful.

Similarly bringing anger and aggression into the home, or cowardice, or laziness, or just a general lack of responsibility – all of these act as a kind of enemy within. And we need to guard against them with as much ferocity as we guard against more obvious threats from the outside. Most acts of self-sabotage need increased self-awareness, self-discipline and determination to change. It'll take a lot of work. But you can do it.

*

Let's Talk About Sex
A powerful example of how to apply this combination of fierce and tender is around sex.

There are few areas in our lives as men where we can get it so spectacularly wrong.

Of course, when men chat about sex, there's a lot of bravado. We've all met top blokey 'shaggers' who think they're God's gift to women. The guys who brag about how many girls they've had, notches on bedposts and belts. They may tell a good story and often enjoy being the envy of the room. However, if you listen carefully, much of what they say is driven by an innate selfishness, and begs the question: I wonder what the women would say? Did they enjoy it? Did it even happen?

Eventually the majority of us figure out the truth: that it's the men who are gentle and generous and giving and tender in bed who make the best lovers. And who are therefore more likely to get most in return.

The Authentic Man knows that selfish pursuit of pleasure for its own sake is self-defeating in the long run.

The role of tenderness in sex should be obvious. But what place has fierceness there?

Here, we come back to that metaphor of the fire. Fire is both useful and dangerous – it needs to be well managed. But it's also romantic. Again, think of candlelit dinners or warm log-fires, or even a simple fireplace at home. As an image, fire has both practical and symbolic power. To manage it well requires discipline and intention.

Discipline in the sense that you have to keep the fire in the grate. If you start spilling the fire of your sex beyond its proper boundaries, you soon discover your house is going up in flames. You might think sprinkling a little fire here or there is just a bit of harmless fun. But most men discover sooner or later that there's no such thing. It doesn't take long before either yourself or others get hurt. Usually both.

Whether we like to admit it or not, sex is about both thinking and feeling. It's far more than the merely physical acts involved. That's why you cannot hope to divorce sex from romance if you actually want to step up and be the Authentic Man in this area of your life.

Can you be fiercely romantic? Have you got the guts to talk about your feelings to the one you love? Have you got the guts to talk about sex with the one you love? Plenty of men do not.

Another way of thinking about this: imagine you have a romantic dinner planned for the evening. Classy restaurant, quality steak, expensive drinks, delicious desserts, with a gorgeous partner. But knowing this, you get up, you have a couple of pastries for breakfast, a McDonalds for lunch and chow down a packet of biscuits with a cup of tea. You've destroyed your appetite for dinner before you've even sat down at the table. Similarly, if you spent your day scrolling through attractive girls on Instagram, or looking at porn, or perving at and flirting with the women in your office, all this is going to reduce your sexual/romantic appetite for your partner when you get home. Masturbating over a woman who isn't your partner is like eating a double Big-Mac before your beautiful steak dinner.

At the end of the day, it's counter-productive. In fact, it's just plain stupid. This may sound harsh, but it's true.

How do we know this?

As we mentioned, we have had thousands of open and honest conversations about the problems that most men face in their lives on the Xtreme Character Challenge weekends which we lead in various remote places around the UK.

In these wild places, men have a space in which they can be vulnerable and unpack a lot of the negative stuff affecting their lives. In just one XCC weekend, we'll hear more conversations about what men are struggling with – in the area of sex especially – than most of us would hear in a decade through our usual friendships. Over the course of a year, these numbers will run into the thousands. With this level of insight, the patterns become very familiar; the same problems come up again and again and again.

So we're talking not only out of our own experience, but that of all the men we have listened to. And countless numbers of those men had marriages and relationships which failed because they were watching porn all the time. They told themselves it's not a problem, that it's under control, that it's got nothing to do with their real-life relationship. And then they act surprised when their life falls apart. Or else they've wandered off into affairs or one-night stands which might easily have been avoided if they had been a bit more fierce with themselves in the first place.

Many would say, 'Well, my relationship went cold. The sex dried up. The fire went out. So I needed this.

I *deserved* this on the side.'

If that is the case, then do something about it now, while you still can.

Tend to your own fire!

Throw on another log, whatever that means for you. We have a part to play as men to keep that fire alight. We need to be fiercely committed to that, fiercely protective of that intimate space. After all, that space is a key distinguishing factor of a connected couple. Having sex together is a core element of what marks that relationship as unique over all the other relationships in your life. We recommend that one of the things that a man who is fierce and tender does is talk tenderly to their partner about their lovemaking. What is good for them? What could be better? What do they need? When a couple is bound together in the mutual service of each other's needs, then the home fire burns bright and warm.

Tend the garden. Fuel the flame. And you'll reap the rewards of a healthy and lasting sexual relationship.

*

The Authentic Man is both fierce AND tender.

Be the guard. Be the gardener. Be strong. Be gentle.

And let everything you do be done with a fierce and tender love.

Chapter Two

RIGHT & WRONG

Imagine you run a business and you employ a number of people. You start work at 8:30am on the dot, and you expect everyone else to do the same. One week, you notice one of the guys in your team gets to his desk an hour late. He does the same the next day, and the next. And he continues to arrive late for the next three weeks. Eventually, at the end of the month, you take him to one side and have it out with him. You tell him that because of his consistent lateness, he's going to penalised. Maybe you cut his pay. Maybe you issue him with a warning. After all, he hasn't worked the hours he should have worked so why should he be rewarded as though he did?

That's only fair, isn't it?

Of course, how you have that conversation is important. You could adopt an official but measured tone. You could be matter-of-fact and to the point. Or you could bawl him out and send him packing with his ears ringing. Each approach is likely to have different consequences. He might suck it up and start turning up on time. Or he could quit and you're left needing to find a replacement.

This all seems straightforward enough. But this approach is lacking something important. At no point have you asked yourself the question:

'WHAT AM I MISSING?'

Now let's imagine the same scenario. You've called them into your office but this time you've started the conversation like this: 'I've noticed you being late for nearly a month now. What's going on?'

Then he starts to explain that his mum has just been diagnosed with cancer. She doesn't have a car, and she asked him to drop her off at the hospital at 9am. It was supposed to only be for four days, but her doctors then said she had to come in for tests every day for the next three weeks. In the meantime, he assures you that he's been working through his lunch break and leaving late after everyone else has gone home...and so on.

Changes the picture, doesn't it?

You're unlikely to respond to his lateness in the same way. In fact, you shouldn't respond in the same way.

Technically, you may have been right to penalise him in the first scenario. It seems pretty black and white to you. But this story shows it's the grey areas that should intrigue us more. Because it's the stuff we don't yet know which will determine how we should respond.

Finding the right path isn't always easy. We often don't know what it looks like. And there are many different angles to consider before concluding something is right or wrong.

It seems to us that this is an area where men can stray into trouble and confusion, often with undesirable consequences. So let's explore this topic some more.

*

The One Who Is Right

The first thing to note is that no one – absolutely no one – is right 100% of the time. If you think you are, then you should probably stop reading this book now and go and write your own book! For the rest of us, sometimes you'll be right; sometimes you'll be wrong. Agreed? Good. Let's move on.

We think this question of being right or wrong is one of the most important areas where the Authentic Man can make a difference in the modern world. We think one of the markers of a healthy man is a man who is able to admit when he is wrong. But even when we are right on a particular point, it doesn't guarantee that we will handle being right well.

Of course most of us like to be right about what we think we know. That's only natural. Few people want to be labelled a fool. But the desire *to be* right is different from the desire *to be seen to be* right. It's often this distinction that trips us up, even when we happen to be correct about something. The truth is sharp as a sword. But it can also be used as a sledgehammer. There are situations when wielding it like a hammer is absolutely the wrong thing to do, and can end up doing a lot more harm than good.

Men love facts. Men are obsessed with being right.

This starts at a very early age. Listen to a group of boys talking: they reel out statistics about their favourite sports hero, their favourite racing car, their favourite wild animal or military hardware. It's no surprise to learn the card game 'Top Trumps' – in which one statistic trumps another – was specifically designed for and targeted at boys. For most men this obsession with facts and being right carries through into adulthood. If you doubt us, just go and listen in on a group of men in a bar. Men can spend hours arguing about which is the best football team or the best car or the best stock in the market, trading facts with each other like blows in a boxing ring. But often these 'facts' are really just opinions dressed up with numbers or big assertions and are often obscurely irrelevant or not worth knowing anyway.

Having said that, the desire for truth is an excellent goal. It's a noble task to set ourselves to – the age-old search for truth, goodness and reliability. Finding truth in life can lead to increased purpose, meaning and fulfilment. Who wouldn't want that? But as we mentioned just above, this desire can easily slip into something far less noble, if not totally ugly: the desire *to be seen to be* the one who is wielding the truth. The hunger to be acknowledged as the one who is right.

*

How Do You Know You Know?
But before we are certain that we hold any truth, we should consider this question: how do we know something is true anyway?

Steven Pinker is a well-known psychologist from Harvard University. On his podcast, *Think With Pinker*, he explores the questions **'What is true?'** and **'How can we know it is true?'** In a recent interview, his Harvard colleague and US district judge Elizabeth Loftus explains how, in a court of law, the language deployed by cross-examining counsel can create a significant difference in a person's testimony, even in eyewitness accounts. For example, a witness in court will give a significantly different answer if the counsel asks, 'How fast do you think the cars were travelling when they *smashed* into each other?' as opposed to, 'How fast do you think the cars were going when they *bumped* into each other?' Frequently, the estimated speed will be significantly higher in response to the first question than the second. But even more than that, using the word 'smash' can draw a statement from the eye-witness that includes things like broken glass or parts of the car on the ground – even when there was none!

Language distorts memory.

So how do you know that you're right, and how can you be sure? Where are you getting your information from when determining that something is true?

When considering these questions, it's vital to remember that our perception of what is true is both *valid* and *flawed*. It is valid because it is your perception (and you are unique), but it is also flawed, because it is just your perception, and you are one of many.

Can you accept that? Can you accept that you don't have a cast-iron grip on the truth? You only have a *perspective* on the truth. Your perspective. Therefore the only reasonable approach to how we handle the truth is one of tempered humility.

But rather than being something that weakens our resolve to know what is right, or do what is right, this understanding can actually give us power and strength to see more. Because holding your opinion lightly enables you to become a lot more curious about the things that you don't know. And what you don't know is quite a lot!

It is understood that wherever you are reading this right now, you are surrounded by approximately 3 billion bits of data. But the average brain is only able to process around 120 bits of data per second. Even if you have an above average brain, you will still struggle to process a fraction of the sounds, noises, senses and data firing off at you right now. So, for all of us, that's a lot of missing information. Lots that we are not seeing.

Of course, we don't notice this much as we go about our day, and as a functionally alert person, you're probably focusing on the most relevant and important bits of data at any given time and making reasonable decisions as you go along. So it's working okay. But what if you are missing something important? What if there is a key piece of data you are overlooking? That is the challenge to all of us: to approach the question of whether I am right or wrong with the necessary dose of humility that makes space for the very real possibility that we may be wrong. Without that, we are likely to get ourselves into trouble.

*

Blind Spots
As we have mentioned, your brain is filtering what you think is true or false all of the time. So much so that you can be literally blind to something that is staring you in the face.

On some speed awareness courses in the UK, they show a video of a group of people passing a basketball between each other. Applicants are told to keep their eye on the ball at all times and count the number of passes between players wearing white shirts. At the end of the clip, they are asked two questions. First: how many passes were made? (Almost everyone gets this number correct.) And the second: did you notice the person dressed up as a gorilla? In its original test, 20 out of 24 psychology students failed to see the person in the gorilla suit. The gorilla was basically invisible to them. The reason: the students were so focused on something else. That's over 80% of a reasonably alert and intelligent control group. After being told what happened, they were asked to watch it a second time and 100% of them spotted the gorilla immediately it came into shot. (You can find this test on YouTube if you want to test this out on your mates.)

So when you are so certain that you are right about something, it is always worth asking yourself:

'WHAT AM I MISSING?'

An important element of this is a phenomenon called 'Cognitive dissonance'. This is when our own view of ourselves is not entirely aligned with how we behave. For example, I may think I'm a reasonable bloke: decent, patient, generally pretty kind. So when someone cuts me up on the road, and I go crazy, that's *their* fault. Or else it's just a momentary lapse at my end. Because I think I'm a nice bloke, not an angry man. Aligned to this is the idea that we tend to judge others by their actions, and ourselves by our intentions. So, again, when driving on the road, if it's me who cuts someone up on the road, it's a reasonable action, because I'm late to pick up my kids from school. But if someone else does it, it's because they're an idiot and a terrible driver. Even though it makes no logical sense, we do this all the time. We excuse ourselves and put the blame elsewhere.

Many people do this, but as men, we struggle especially with this type of behaviour. We don't like being wrong. We find it deeply uncomfortable. Maybe because we think it says something about our competence as a man. Maybe for a lot of reasons, conscious and subconscious.

So we hope that by now, you are convinced that even when you feel 100% sure of your perspective, from a purely theoretical point of view, there is a very good chance that you are still missing something important which may change your position. Even so, happily, sometimes you will actually be right! You really will know your stuff, and you will have reliable evidence to back it up. But here is another layer to consider: in order to thrive and be the good guy we think we are, there are times, even when we are right, that it's preferable not to show that you're right. This can be hard to do. It's often uncomfortable to allow someone else to take credit for our thinking. We often find it hard to go at the pace of someone less mentally agile than us. It can be painful to let an opinion or a 'fact' that you strongly disagree with go unchallenged. But you don't want to be that guy who always has to be right. People soon get sick of men being so sure of themselves. Arrogance is not a great look. And the result is that, sooner or later, people move away from you. It's hard to stick around someone like that.

In any dispute or argument, there are right and wrong ways of behaving. You can be right and still act badly, as much as you can be wrong and act well.

Responsibility

It breaks down something like this:

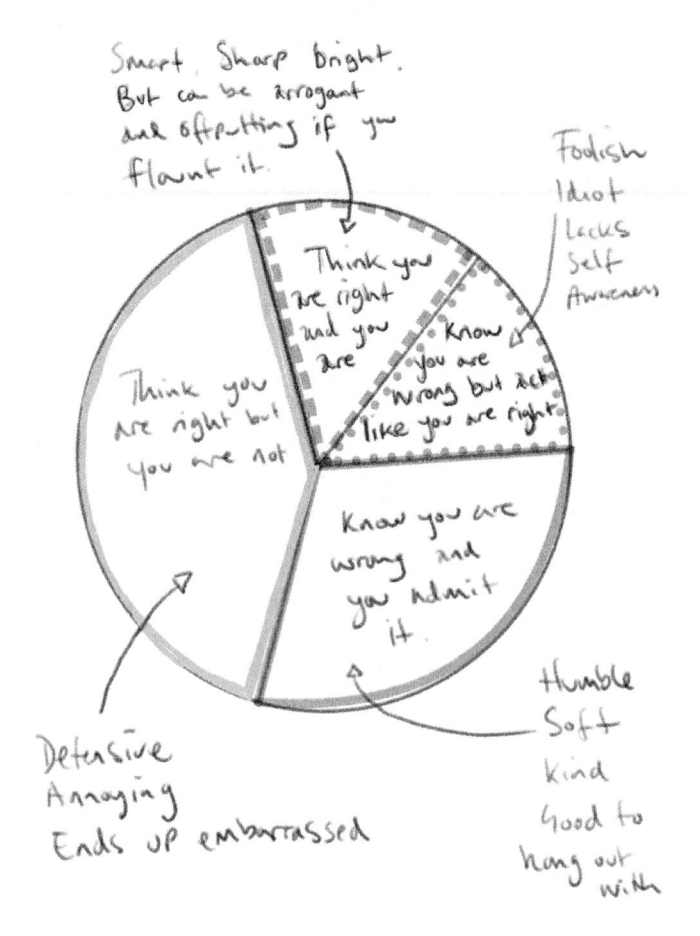

Handwritten pie chart with four quadrants and annotations:

- *Top-left quadrant* ("Think you are right and you are"): Smart, Sharp, bright. But can be arrogant and offputting if you flaunt it.
- *Top-right quadrant* ("Know you are wrong but act like you are right"): Foolish, Idiot, Lacks Self Awareness
- *Left quadrant* ("Think you are right but you are not"): Defensive, Annoying, Ends up embarrassed
- *Bottom-right quadrant* ("Know you are wrong and you admit it"): Humble, Soft, Kind, Good to hang out with

Almost every argument or dispute can fit into one of these four quadrants:

1) You think you're right, and you are.
2) You think you're right, and you're not.
3) You know you're wrong, but pretend you're right.
4) You know you're wrong, and you admit it.

The question is, how should you act in each case? Let's look at these in turn.

*

You Think You're Right, And You Are:
As we've said, there are situations in life when being right is still wrong. When winning an argument can mean losing a whole lot more.

Having to be right *all the time* is not a winning strategy. When someone is described as 'always needing to be right' it's rarely meant as a compliment and usually comes at the cost of the trust and respect of those around them.

Most of us can instinctively think of situations when this is the case. And yet, isn't it so easy to find ourselves drawn into disagreements that don't actually serve anyone? Pride, pressure, power play, performance, our perception of ourselves and of others can all provoke the wrong response in us, even if we happen to be right.

And often, even when we think we've won an argument, it may be that the other person has conceded just to keep the peace, or else they've fallen back into a place of silent resentment. It's rare that, even when we're right, we actually manage to convince someone to change their mind, especially if we approach a disagreement or conflict with the wrong attitude. An attitude that makes no allowance for listening to the other person, or that is open to the possibility that we may in fact be wrong.

Few things are less attractive than someone who asserts the truth in a very domineering way. So being right is one thing. Behaving right at the same time is another. And arguably more important.

So we always need to be self-aware, asking ourselves, 'Do I need to be right in this context?'

Muddling these issues creates a trap that, as men, we fall into again and again. But finding the right balance can have a hugely positive impact on the world around us too.

That said, we are not suggesting that there is never a moment when we should stand up for the truth – or at least what we believe to be the truth. There often is. Stand in your power as a man, as a father, as a husband, as a business leader, team member, friend or whatever. That is important, too. But we need wisdom to ask ourselves when we are just trying to win an argument for our own sake and when we are honestly and genuinely trying to do the right thing. And even then, if the situation calls for us to stick to our guns, can we do it with humility, a listening attitude and respect for the other person?

*

You Think You're Right, And You're Not
Humility is again key in this situation, as well as a willingness to listen to others around you who might know better.

The two of us were driving many years ago in Pisa, Italy, with our wives. This was in the early days of Sat-Nav, long before google maps. People were just getting used to following a Sat-Nav, and it wasn't always clear which way the little arrow was directing you to turn. There could also be a bit of a lag while the arrow caught up with your real position.

Right & Wrong

We were driving back from a restaurant when James hit a roundabout and saw the Sat-Nav taking us right. He decided to go straight on.

His wife Emiko asked what he was doing.

'This is a quicker way,' he said. 'The Sat-Nav is taking us a slow route.' It wanted to take us down a dual carriageway. We were now climbing up a steep hill, the road was getting narrower.

The screen still hadn't adjusted to our new route. 'Just wait a second,' James assured us. 'It'll see where we are going soon and take time off our route.'
'Why don't you just turn around and go back the way it was telling us to go?' asked Emiko.
'Yeah, man,' agreed Myles. 'Just turn in this guy's driveway.'
At that moment, the Sat-Nav finally made its adjustment.
'You've just added eleven minutes to our route, James,' said Becs, with only a trace of sarcasm.

But James was undeterred. 'Nah, that thing must be wrong,' he said confidently, while we looked glumly at the massive detour the computer was now taking us on. By this stage we had gone so far the wrong way that it really didn't make any difference if we turned back or just carried on James' route.

So on we went, all feeling annoyed at James. Now, in this case James sincerely believed he knew better than the computer. He hadn't taken us on a long detour for fun. He thought he was right, but he wasn't. In the end, he did admit his mistake and apologised. If only he'd asked himself, 'What am I missing?' we might have got there quicker. You'd

59

think three other adults and a computer all saying differently might have given him a clue.

By insisting he was right to save face among the rest of us, in fact he'd only lost it.

*

You Know You're Wrong, But Pretend You're Right.
When Myles was just starting out as a plumber, he was working on a house refurbishment project for a customer who also happened to be a friend. This friend had told Myles that he worked as a project manager for a large building company in west London. He claimed to have tons of experience overseeing large and complex development projects, so the refurbishment of his own house should be, for him, a piece of cake.

In other words, he presented Myles and the other tradesmen on the job with a bravado image that he knew best. So, when it came to Myles' plumbing piece of the project, it was the client who ordered all the bathroom furniture and equipment that was needed. But when Myles tried to install what he had ordered, he found he couldn't figure it out at all.

Nothing seemed to work. He became so stumped that he asked his dad for help. His dad immediately identified the problem: the client had ordered the wrong kit. But Myles said that was impossible because the guy had so much experience. Surely he wouldn't make so basic a mistake as ordering a toilet with a waste pipe so low the water was expected to run uphill? When Myles went to him and suggested there was a problem, instead of hearing him out the client told him, 'Find a solution.'

Myles soon discovered he wasn't the only person struggling to work with him, however. One by one, the other tradesmen on the job came to Myles and asked him what this guy really did for a living. Because their wives were friends, Myles told them what he knew: that he was a project manager for a large development company. But the others just laughed at that. 'No way he's a project manager. He doesn't know what he's talking about.'

As the job continued more and more mistakes materialised, all attributable to this guy's certainty that he knew best when it was becoming painfully clear that he did not. Myles was still new to plumbing, so he was less willing to call him out on it, but the other tradesmen were old timers and were much more confident in pointing out the client's mistakes. But when confronted, especially in front of other people, rather than admit his mistakes, he'd just brazen it out, and tell them all to fix the problem, often blaming the tradesmen for his own mistakes. The result was very negative. Apart from the time and money wasted doing things 'his' way and then having to fix them, Myles watched as one by one, the entire project team lost all respect for him. Eventually one of the other tradesmen called the company he claimed to project manage for and found out that, on these 'massive projects' he bragged about, all he did were the CAD designs for the kitchens! He had never once worked on site. In other words, he had zero practical experience.

Presumably he had reasoned that if he styled it out as someone with way more experience than he had, it would bolster his credibility and therefore his authority over the project team and so he would get more out of them. But the actual result was that he soon lost authority as well as their respect. He would have done far better, once mistakes became apparent, to listen more and be a little humbler about the level of his experience compared to the others on site.

The irony is that if the guy had adopted the exact opposite approach, his project team's view of him would have risen rather than dwindled to nothing. Imagine if he'd said, 'This is the first project I've managed, I'm not 100% sure of what I'm doing. Maybe this would work. What do you think?' Immediately you're calling the best out of someone, aren't you? Inviting them to step up and give you their best answer to any problem.

Sure, there is a view that you can 'fake it till you make it.' But if you are 100% faking it, and you know it, sooner or later the rubber is going to hit the road, and you'll be found out.

The mistake that this client/friend made in Myles' story was that he overplayed the reputational risk of coming clean about his lack of experience. In fact, he not so much overplayed it as completely miscalculated it. Adopting the strategy he did proved to be catastrophic to his reputation among his project team. By the end of the job, they despised him.

He was wrong and he knew it, but he pretended to be right.

For some reason, as men, we think we are supposed to know everything. But as we have seen in the opening section of this chapter, due to the functional limitations of our brain, we can't possibly hope to know everything. So we might as well admit that fact and move on, rather than protecting our reputations like a fragile house of cards, the collapse of which only threatens to be more painful the higher we build them.

And since no one is right 100% of the time, let's look at a better way to behave when we are in the wrong.

*

You Know You're Wrong, And You Admit It
Everyone makes mistakes.

We screw up; we offend people; we fly off the handle. We muck things up; we tell white lies; we're sneaky; we cut corners. Sometimes we do things we know are totally wrong. We steal; we cheat on our wives and girlfriends; we break the law; we kick our dogs; we get too drunk; we get too high. We swear and curse at complete strangers; we betray our friends.

Everyone makes mistakes.

Whether what we've done is trivial and of little consequence or something earth-shatteringly terrible and painful to the people around us – the first step towards the resolution of our mistakes is always the same:

Admitting that we're wrong.

That is true whether we're talking about something being morally wrong or factually wrong. Either way, a willingness to own up is the quickest way to a good outcome.

Think back to the gorilla experiment in the speed awareness test. It's okay that we are blind to certain things that may be really obvious to everyone else. That's inevitable. We can only operate out of our own perception. And we can't focus on everything all at once. But once something becomes clear to us, something that alters how we see things, we need to have the humility and wisdom to change our position.

After all, we can't even be sure that we have a true and accurate view of our own self.

Think about how you view yourself.

Are you a kind, reasonable, calm and patient man? Or are your children scared of your temper flare-ups? Do your work colleagues think you're moody and irritable? Do your sports teammates think you're a bit on the aggressive side?

It's easy to compartmentalize our lives and fail to piece together the bigger picture. But there are usually themes running through all these different arenas. And what they have in common says something significant about you.

How many unseen gorillas are walking through our lives right now? Walking through our marriages and families, through our friendship groups and businesses, through our communities and culture? Gorillas all over the place. Some of us might see some of them while others of us are completely blind to them. No one can see them all. That is why we need each other. We all have something to learn from one another.

The perception of others may be a slightly distorted mirror from which to figure out who we really are, but it is a mirror nonetheless. And we would do well to pay attention to what we can see in it.

For example, James likes to think of himself as a bit of a gentleman. He tries to be polite, tries to be courteous. He plays the diplomat in certain relationships. He smooths things out when there's a problem. He's a fixer. He thinks of himself as a caring and careful man.

But the reality is he's not a 'gentle' man. He breaks stuff. Sometimes he's too rough with his two boys.

He tightens screws too much so they snap. He can be clumsy. He is hasty. He rips stuff out and does more damage than was there before. He can be careless with his words, and that can be painful for others. And he often doesn't care. He thinks, 'Oh well, I did my best. If I break something, we can figure out a way round it later.' So maybe a truer perception of James is that he's actually a bit of a ruthless man who needs to take far more care than he does, both with people and with things.

Let's take a step back for a moment.

Even as the authors of this book, we ourselves have to admit the same is true when it comes to everything that we are sharing with you in these pages. Our advice and suggestions are true, according to the way we see it and to the best of our ability to express our thinking. We mean everything we say, honestly and sincerely. But we are the first to admit that we might be missing something. Undoubtedly we are. And we have to be willing to admit that we don't have all the answers, nor do we have the last word on any of this stuff. In fact, we would like anyone reading this book to get in touch with us about anything they don't agree with or think that we have got wrong or overlooked. We mean it! Our email address is at the back of the book.

We are on a journey as much as you are. We want to learn. And hopefully through that willingness to learn we might get closer to the truth as time goes on.

So a willingness to admit when you are wrong is key.

*

Grow Humility
Look at the four sections of our quadrant again. Most of us will see that we fall into each one of the them at different times and in different circumstances in our life. But we hope you can see there's a healthy way and a unhealthy way to behave in each case.

Take a look at where you spend most of your time.

We hope that the overarching message of this chapter helps grow greater humility within all of us. As the author CS Lewis put it, 'Humility is not thinking less of yourself, but thinking of yourself less.' When you do that, you start to appreciate that the world is a big place, much bigger than your own individual perspective can encompass. That is why we need each other. It helps us to see more, and together we might feel our way forward towards truth, towards greater meaning, purpose and fulfilment in our lives.

The Authentic Man develops the habit of asking these questions:

'What am I missing?'

'What do you think?'

Chapter Three

SORRY & FORGIVING

Forgiveness is one of the most defining concepts in a man's life. How he applies this virtue will determine the kind of man that he will become. In fact, it is such a powerful concept, the same is true for all humans, cultures and nations.

As Nelson Mandela famously said, 'resentment is like drinking poison and then hoping it will kill your enemies.' What he's saying is that, in the end, refusing to forgive someone does more harm to you than to your enemies. In contrast, Mandela also said, 'Forgiveness liberates the soul, it removes fear. That's why it's such a powerful weapon.'

It is no accident that by adopting this attitude towards the wrongs that had been done to his people, Mandela managed to navigate South Africa through a political minefield that could have ended in a never-ending bloodbath. Instead his policy of Truth & Reconciliation meant that the historic wrongs done to the black population in South Africa were publicly acknowledged, confronted, apologised for, and forgiven, and the country was able to move on into a period of genuine freedom.

On the other hand, you only have to look at other cultures where tit-for-tat blood feuds, unforgiveness and resentment are the norm to see how wrong things can go. The Balkan Wars of the 1990s are just one example, where the grievances between different ethnic groups could be traced back a hundred years or more. In places like Iraq and Syria, the sectarian violence continues to this day.

At the level of the individual, we think that the

Authentic Man needs to be sorry more often and more readily – meaning he takes responsibility for the wrongs that he has done. And at the same time, he is open to forgiveness when someone else has done him wrong.

Perhaps more than in any other area which we discuss, the choices we make about being sorry and being forgiving will determine the kind of man we are becoming, and ultimately the legacy that we will leave behind.

*

The Problem Of Selfishness
First of all, we have to face up to a cold, hard fact that we are born into selfishness. Different worldviews might give different explanations for why this is, but we don't think it is controversial to say: humans are intrinsically selfish. Both men and women; children and adults. Every day we are doing things that are focused on serving our own interests, and not focused on serving the interests of others. When this happens, some may be in the wrong, some in the right. As we have said, often it is not even 100% clear which is which. But, frighteningly, sometimes it is clear. And the person in the wrong is us.

Yet how often, even when we know we have done wrong, do we still believe that we don't need to be sorry because of the bad things that have happened to us in the past. We load the scales of justice in our favour. We think that because I have been the victim of wrongs in the past, I'm excused to dole out a few wrongs of my own as well almost like the wrongs done to you are credit in the bank. When we do this we assume the identity of victimhood, and this identity gives us licence to bite back.

*

The Choice Of Victimhood
Often, when we feel hurt or wounded, we cry out, 'Why do bad things happen to good people?'

It's a natural, gut-level question of human existence. And there's no easy answer.

But the fact is, bad things do happen to good people. Bad things also happen to bad people.

The rain falls on the good and the bad. The sun shines on the good and the bad. Our own moral standing doesn't seem to affect that at all. But what does affect the consequences of what happens to us is the attitude we carry.

One response to the bad things we have experienced in our lives is to assume the identity of victimhood. We think of victimhood literally as being like a physical hood. So when the rain comes, you throw it up over your head. You may feel more protected from the rain, but this also narrows your perspective, dulling your senses to the world around you, and it often overwhelms you with a sense of self-pity at the things that you have suffered.

By the way, we are sorry for those things. We don't like that they have happened to you. We don't like that they happen to anyone. But such is the reality of life. Bad things have happened to you. Bad things have happened to us. Yours might be worse. Ours might be worse. The difference between us is in fact irrelevant because the same choice confronts us both: what are we going to do about it?

In her international bestselling book called *The Choice*, psychologist Edith Eger talks a lot about victimhood. Her story is remarkable. In 1944, as a sixteen-year-old, Edith was sent to the Nazi death camp at Auschwitz. There she endured unimaginable experiences, including being made to dance for the infamous Josef Mengele on the very night her mother was murdered in a nearby gas chamber. Over the coming months, Edith's bravery helped her sister to survive, and led to her bunkmates rescuing her during a death march. When their camp was finally liberated, Edith was pulled from a pile of bodies by an American GI, barely alive. She had a broken back, typhoid fever, pneumonia and pleurisy. By any standards of human suffering, her story of surviving Auschwitz must rank as one of the worst. Witnessing her parents, friends and fellow Jews being systematically annihilated, living in terror of her life for five years of her youth, enduring starvation, disease, cold, and the horrors of what she saw – these are things beyond our imagination. And yet, Edith explains in her book how she would not allow that trauma to become the defining experience of her life. She would not allow herself to remain a prisoner of her own past.

Rather, she talks openly about what you need to do to unlock your own freedom. To truly live free from the wrongs that were done to you, however bad these may be. Her main point has to do with making your own choices.

You have the power to choose.

The keys to your freedom are in your own pocket. So choose what you think, choose what you believe. Choose what you listen to and who you listen to. Choose what you allow in and choose what you keep out.

If you have the hood of a victim identity pulled up over your ears, wandering around feeling nothing but pity for yourself, often you are not making a choice at all. Or rather, you are choosing by default, by inaction. Those bad things that happened to you will affect you and go on affecting you for as long as you let them.

Edith Eger thinks that time alone does not heal. It's what you do with the time that counts. So, she explains, merely hoping the effects of what you have suffered will go away in time is not a real choice. That is passivity. She asserts again and again that you must make a choice. That is what is important.

(Hence the title of her book.)

And after all, she should know. If she could do this, then there is no reason that we should not also be able to do the same.

*

The Paradox Of Choice
Often, our problem living in the West in the 21st century is not having limited choices, but having rather too many of them. There is a paradox: being overwhelmed with too many choices leads to paralysis. Too many paths at a crossroads and we end up taking none of them. We freeze and refuse to choose.

Clearly, one way of avoiding this problem is to narrow your choices according to your values. So, for example, if according to your values, you have already decided that divorce is not an option for you and your spouse, then however bad it gets between you, you have already agreed that you *have* to find a way forward together. This helps you. It changes your approach to dealing with your marital problems since you've at least removed the option of running away from them.

Decide what your values are.

What do you believe is important? Telling the truth? Being faithful? Helping others when you can? Loyalty among friends? Being generous? Being honest in your business dealings? We all put greater or lesser weight on these and many other values.

How about this one:

Do you believe the basic idea that there is good in the world?

In which case, you can choose to be good and not bad.

Do you think it's important to have freedom from the brokenness of the past? If so, choose that.

Narrow your choices.

Pick a road and then walk down it.

*

Being Sorry
What should we be sorry for then?

If you can choose freedom even though bad things have happened to you, then this begs the question, why should you be sorry?

There's an old saying: the heart of the human problem is the problem of the human heart. We have to look inside ourselves to recognise how complicated the problem of good and evil truly is. The Soviet dissident writer Alexander Solzhenitsyn wrote this: 'If only it were all so simple! If only there were evil people somewhere insidiously committing evil deeds, and it were necessary only to separate them from the rest of us and destroy them. *But the line dividing good and evil cuts through the heart of every human being.*' [our emphasis]

Our selfishness (and the bad that often comes from it) is baked into us. It is present everywhere and in all of us. It pollutes and worms its way into our lives, unrelenting. It never stops. There is no internal solution to the effects of selfishness. It has to come from outside of you.

This is something that Alcoholics Anonymous programme recognises. (As does Narcotics Anonymous.) We are big advocates of these programmes and think they offer powerful insights into how to deal with this problem of our innate selfishness.

Famously, the AA programme consists of Twelve Steps. The first three are crucial to overcoming the effects of your own selfishness:

1) Admit your weakness;
2) Recognise you are powerless over it; and
3) Acknowledge your need for help to change.

This is the crux of the transformation that comes from following the AA programme and others like it.

So when looking at what in our lives we should be

sorry for, acknowledging that we, like everyone else, are essentially selfish, is a good place to start. We are sorry for our own brokenness, our own pre-disposition towards selfishness. We recognise that is a basic reality within us. We are unhappy with it. We want to change. We want to participate in driving that change.

This is the essential flow.

And it follows that a part of being sorry, of wanting to change, is recognising that other people are made of the same selfish fabric as you. We are all fallible human beings. We make mistakes. We do things we shouldn't do. We hurt and we fail each other. Because of this, we should be open to forgiving other people, in the same way that we would want them to be open to forgiving us.

Make sense?

*

Defining Sorry
We identify three different levels of being sorry. These are:

1) *Sorry, not sorry.* Essentially paying lip service to an apology but not meaning it and not regretting what you have done.
2) *Sorry, I did the best I could.* This still falls short of taking full responsibility for your actions. It expresses regret at the outcome more than remorse at your part in causing any hurt.
3) *Sorry, that was my fault. And I don't ever want to do that again.* This is where you are genuinely sorry for the hurt/damage you have caused. You acknowledge that and take responsibility for it. Even

more, you want to make amends and change your behaviour so that you don't cause the same hurt again.

Most of us are so used to experiencing the first level of 'Sorry, not sorry' that it is easy to become cynical about apologies in general. Too often we hear politicians on our TVs and radios picking their way around public apologies with language that carefully avoids admitting their own culpability and refuses to take responsibility on their own shoulders. And on a much more basic level, many of us will repeat this phrase time and time again throughout the day with no thought about the actual sentiment behind the words, and no intention of changing.

How many of us have trotted out, 'I'm sorry, Miss" to our teachers at school, only to be told 'You're not sorry. You're just sorry you got caught'? It's the same instinct. We roll out apologies just to get ourselves off the hook, not because we really care or have any intention to change our behaviour or want to do things any differently in the future.

Two days before they were due to fly to India for what they thought would be a permanent move, Myles and his wife Becs had a wedding to go to. The bride was Becs' closest childhood friend. The wine being served was high end, and Myles realised this was also the last time he would see some of their friends and family for a long time. Consequently, he got, in his words, 'sozzled and emotional'.' During the speeches he was loudly crying and laughing and drinking. After the speeches it was time for photos with the bridesmaids (Becs was one) with husbands and so on. Myles vaguely remembers crying and telling all his friends how much he loved them and how much he was going to miss them. Needless to say the photos are of Becs looking radiant and Myles flushed and puffy-eyed from crying.

The next morning he apologised for his behaviour to the bride and groom. He wasn't saying, 'Sorry, I'll never do that again;' more, 'Sorry I made a tit of myself and ruined the photos.' He was also supposed to put the bride and groom's bags in their car, but forgot. He was sorry for that too, but also couldn't promise that wouldn't happen again.

For James, something similar is true in the way he drives. When a policeman pulls him over and tells him he's been driving too fast, he'll take the reprimand on the chin and apologise to the officer. But he's not actually that sorry, and he's not going to make any lasting changes to the way he drives either.

But what if something bad did happen? It's not a pleasant thought. He knows he has consistent form on this, but something in him still refuses to change. (There's that innate selfishness we talked about.) He doesn't know why. The shame of it is that it would probably take a serious accident or unfortunate event to make him genuinely sorry for speeding and thereby cause him to change his behaviour.

A sheepish kind of sorry for getting drunk at a party or for getting caught speeding is not the kind of sorry we are advocating for here. We are trying to encourage – in ourselves and in you – a sorry which demands a 180-degree turn. In military language, an 'about-turn'.' Where you were marching in one direction, but now you turn around and start walking back the opposite way.

Now, if we are serious about being sorry for the

things we do wrong in our lives, then what is that we are going to have to walk away from?

Sometimes we need a hard lesson in life to show us exactly what that is.

In the first few years after Myles qualified as a plumber, it was not unusual for him to tell customers to 'do one' over the phone – usually when he was tired and frustrated and they were being annoying. Typical tradesman. Still, that was no excuse. At one point, his mother-in-law overheard him speaking to a customer in this less than respectful tone, and when he put the phone down, she said, 'You were a bit sharp with that person on the phone, weren't you?'
'Oh, I get a dozen calls like that every week from really annoying people time wasting or just trying to get some advice,' returned Myles casually.
'Hmm, you were rather rude, I thought! That might bite you back one day if you don't watch out.'

Myles being Myles, he didn't take this sound advice to heart. Instead, life was going to have to teach him his lesson the hard way.

A while later, he received a call from a lady with a haggy voice who had found his business number online, asking him if he could come round and check her gas supply and meter, which seemed to be faulty. Since he was already booked up for the week, and knew he was on holiday the week after, he wasn't very interested in the old lady's business. The lady, however, continued to explain her problem. As she went on, it seemed clear to Myles that she simply needed to put some more money in her meter and she would have her gas supply back on. But she was adamant the problem was more complicated than that and she wanted him to come round in person to take a look.

'How much do you charge for a call out?' she asked.
'Seventy-five pounds plus VAT,' Myles replied.
'Seventy-five pounds! That's daylight robbery, that is. What are you, some kind of cowboy?'
Reaching the limit of his patience at this point, Myles informed her, somewhat unchivalrously, that she could 'just go f—k herself.'
'I beg your pardon,' she squawked.
'You heard me, love. I said, "go f—k yourself."'

Then he put the phone down.

Sorted, he thought. Bloody annoying people. No respect for the trades.

A few seconds passed before his phone rang again. It was the same lady. 'I can't believe you just spoke to me like that, young man. I'm going to call trading standards and Check-a-Trade and Google and everything...You haven't heard the end of this.'

As it happens, this was a towering understatement.

It took a few hours of reflection for Myles to think maybe he had acted a little harshly and unwisely, and that he had overstepped the mark.

He certainly didn't want this woman calling up those places blackening his name. So, he decided to call her back.

'Hello, is that Mrs. Tapper?' (Not her real name.)
'Yes? Well it's Sid Dhillon here,' he said in a gruff voice much deeper than his own.

Responsibility

'I'm the manager of Dhillon Plumbers and understand one of the lads was a bit rude to you earlier this morning. I wanted to clear up any – erm – slight offence he may have caused.' Genius, Myles thought, pretending it's the boss giving one of the apprentices a ticking off. Smooth it all over. She'll be right as rain.

'Slight offence! He told me to go—'
'Yes, he did explain,' 'Sid' jumped in.
'How can we make this right?'

What was finally arranged was that 'Sid' would send around someone to look at her meter the following week. Although Myles had zero intention of following through on the call-out and assumed Mrs. Tapper would get fed up with calling his voicemail while he was away on holiday and find another company.

But this is not what happened. Instead, having turned off his phone during his week away, he returned to England to discover that Mrs. Tapper had left at least half a dozen voicemails of escalating fury on his phone. It seemed she had discovered his plumbing business was a single person company and that 'Sid' was in truth the very same person who had told her so categorically where she could go.

What followed is too long-winded to go into in much detail. Suffice to say, Mrs. Tapper's quest for justice to see this man exposed for the foul-mouthed brute that he undoubtedly had appeared, was merciless and far-reaching. By the time she was done, Myles had been struck off Check-a-Trade; and his Facebook community, his in-laws, his church leaders, and his wife had all been contacted and told exactly what kind of monster lurked in their midst. She even contacted the Bishop of Chichester. Only God knows why. But she did.

What appeared to Myles at first as an absurd over-reaction ended up being quite traumatic for him. The relentless campaign to blacken his name and reputation among pretty much everyone who knew him, whether in a personal or professional capacity, went on for some months. He never knew when Mrs. Tapper was going to strike next. Even his attempts to reach out and apologise to her directly, and appeal to any sense of mercy in her, were turned back against him: an email of apology was simply published on Facebook as proof of admission to his crimes and evidence that he was indeed a liar. Myles' wife Becs found out about the whole ordeal when the woman contacted her directly on Facebook to tell her what a toad of a man she is married too. Myles hadn't yet told her, because he thought the whole thing would just go away.

Myles wants to just add that this really was one of the truly low points of his life. He genuinely thought this would spell the end of his business and that this woman would not stop until she had made sure of it.

Essentially there was nothing he could do to solve the problem. He tried everything. He just had to let the consequences of his mistake play themselves out in the most hideously public way.

To make matters worse, at a certain point during Mrs. Tapper's campaign, Myles' softly spoken mother-in-law did point out that she had in fact warned him not to be so sharp with his customers on the phone, and how he might have avoided all this trouble.

Responsibility

'Humility comes from humiliation,' intoned his father-in-law over her shoulder, always ready with some wise aphorism.

By then, Myles had certainly suffered sufficient humiliation to emerge a humbler, meeker man.

The consequence of all this is why we tell you this story. Having never taken very seriously the notion that, if provoked, it was bad to be rude to customers (or indeed anyone), Myles was now feeling the heavy weight of remorse. He had climbed out of the valley of the 'sorry, not sorry' level of apology, merely to cover his back, into the morally-improving uplands of genuine regret, remorse and responsibility. Through the pain of being forced to face the consequences of his own actions, extreme though they were, he at last arrived at a point where he resolved never to be rude to customers like that again.

Since then, he has endured customers far more annoying or rude to him than Mrs. Tapper and kept his mouth firmly shut.

We hope this remains the case.

This is what we mean when we say being truly sorry means making a 180-degree turn. Walking away from the habits and behaviour that we know to be wrong or to cause harm. (In this case, both to others and to ourselves.)

Often we know the things we do wrong. We just don't want to turn away from them.

At least, in Myles' case, his humiliation did lead to a genuine sorry. But we want to help you avoid having to learn in such an exposing way.

Even for those things we think we are going to get away with, his story is a lesson about how discoverable you are in this day and age. Cheating, dishonesty, fraud, rudeness, rage, violence. We can be exposed for it all very easily these days. Better to face whatever it is now in the quiet of your own conscience than in the court of public opinion, which is rarely sympathetic.

Myles had been an idiot. He was completely in the wrong. He'd got away with it before. It's just that this time he had upset the wrong person. For the rest of us, we never know who that is going to be. So all the more reason to turn around now.

Real sorry may come from regret; it may come from humiliation. It doesn't really matter. The most important marker of being truly sorry is the desire that it will *not* happen again. If we were walking towards it, now we are walking away from it.

Of course, we are still human. We are still weak. We cannot guarantee that it will never happen again. But at least we are trying to escape that cycle of behaviour, rather than rolling along with it.

*

Taking Responsibility
Being sorry recognises your part in something that happened. It's about taking responsibility – as is much of the advice that we share in this book. It is not just an acknowledgement that the outcome went badly; it is also about acknowledging that you played a part in bringing about that outcome.

We should bear the consequence of our own actions. And sometimes these arise as a result of an honest mistake, sometimes, a dishonest one. We think we should own the consequences whatever the moral component within it.

This feeds into our next story.

This book was almost never written.

We came up with the idea of it in the summer of 2017 when we were on holiday together. At that time, we did everything together. We ran XCC weekends together. We partied together. We spoke several times on the phone each week together. We made each other godparents to our children. We did everything but cut our hands and swear blood brotherhood.

We were 100% convinced that we would be close friends like this forever. As far as we were concerned, this friendship would never die. And yet, within a month of saying that to each other on this holiday, suddenly we were never going to speak again.

Now, at this point, we have to explain that although we will continue to be open and honest with you, we're not going to go into the same level of detail with this story as we did with others. The reason for this is because insensitive repetition of the detail caused much of the trouble in the first place. (It took a long, long time for James, in particular, to realise this.)

So let's see if we can convey enough to illustrate the point.

In essence this was about James' mistake in not taking seriously enough someone else's pain; and not taking into account that just because he couldn't see something, did not mean that it wasn't there. And that it was not absolutely real to the other person.

You've probably seen a hundred movies in which the protagonist makes a miscalculation or a mistake at the beginning, and then spends much of the rest of the movie trying to rectify that mistake over and over again. But all they are doing is digging themselves into a deeper hole. It's only when they stop trying to control the situation according to their old way of doing things that they might actually learn the lesson they need to learn, make the necessary change, and so get themselves out of the hole.

What happened between James and Myles ran along similar lines.

Myles shared a personal story with James. James underestimated the depth of the underlying issue, and after the passage of some time, assuming everything was sufficiently in the past, he did something which, had he really been paying attention and been open to the sensitivities at play, he never would have done.

The rupture was severe. Trust was broken. The friendship was over. All the while, James struggled to understand the reaction. He'd been slung out in the cold, and he didn't like it.

James being James, he thought he could fix the situation. But fixing it meant involving other people.

And each time that James thought he had now solved the problem, he discovered he had only made it worse.

His incomprehension was genuine and honest in that sense. He just couldn't grasp that, in spite of all his good intentions, the result was the end of this friendship that was very precious to him.

Eventually another friend who was close to Myles came to James and tried to explain the perspective from Myles' side. He asked James to imagine someone walking down a dark alley at night. A large man carrying a bat approaches from the other end, all the while calling out, 'Don't worry, I'm not going to hurt you. I'm not going to hurt you.' Such words are hardly reassuring. If the man really wanted to reassure the other person that he was no threat, he would turn around or stop walking altogether.

'Can you see that you're that guy?' the friend asked.

'You're walking towards him with a bat in your hand saying, "I'm not going to hurt you, I'm not going to hurt you." But really you're just making things worse.'

At this stage, James was still in the second type of sorry. *Sorry, but I did the best I could.* Or perhaps more accurately, *Sorry...but I still don't get it.*

It took a long time, even from this point, for him to see how painful his actions had been. A more considerate friend would have just known better. The whole sorry episode had exposed something in James that is both his strength and also his flaw: his ability to talk. His mouth can be his greatest asset, but their fall-out had proved that it could also be his greatest liability. In this case, his mouth couldn't solve the situation. He just had to shut up for a while. For him, that was a hard lesson to accept.

Part of what eventually brought reconciliation between them was a narrowing of choices – as we mentioned at the start of this chapter. Both Myles and James, deep down, had made a commitment that, as bad as this seemed to be, it would not mean the death of their friendship forever. They weren't just going to walk away. Somehow, with humility and time, they were determined that the friendship would survive.

But the rift between them was real. And the only way to heal the rift was being truly sorry on one side, and able to forgive on the other.

*

What is forgiveness?
Forgiveness does not mean forgive and forget. It means forgive and remember. When you wound someone else, the wound may heal. But it leaves a scar. The scar is that memory.

We can't undo the things we've done wrong. We have to face the consequences of our actions, as we've said. But we can be sorry, and we can demonstrate the reality of our remorse by making a commitment never to scar someone else in the same way again.

But if you are the one who is scarred? What then?

The author C.S. Lewis wrote, 'Everyone says forgiveness is a lovely idea, until they have something to forgive.'

No doubt we've all experienced the truth of this many times in our lives.

No one says forgiveness is easy. It's not. It's very costly. But it is also worth that cost. What we win through forgiveness is so much more valuable than what we stand to gain by refusing to forgive.

Remember: *Time does not heal, it's what you do with that time that counts.*

While James had to go away and figure out that what he had to do was stop trying to fix the situation, Myles spent that time processing his pain and also his response to what James had done. It's not enough for the wounded party to pull up the drawbridge and barricade themselves inside their fortress of self-righteousness, bitterness and self-pity. At least not if they want to move forward in life. They, too, have the power to make choices. Not just the choice to resist being a victim, but to be a reconciler, too.

'Blessed are the peace-makers.'

And those blessings become very real to those able to forgive.

There came a moment some months after the worst of the rift had died down that we were able to sit down on a grassy hilltop and chat through what had happened. When James could say – and absolutely mean it – 'I'm sorry.' And Myles could reply, 'I forgive you.' In fact, he also offered an apology for how harshly James had been treated at times.

Reconciliation came.

But neither of us will forget.

*

The Reason For This Book
This book has been written out of the brokenness of that event.

As we've said, we had already been talking about writing a book together before this all blew up between us. But during it, both of our wives lost a lot of faith in us and rightly so. Our credibility as two authentic men who had something significant to say was seriously compromised. Who were we to think we had anything valid to say to other men, about masculinity or anything else, if we could screw up our friendship this badly?

They had a good point.

Who were we?

That was the challenge for us from that time onward. To think long and hard about what it really means to be the Authentic Man. A big part of it is humility, taking responsibility, and the realisation that all too often we, from our limited individual perspectives, are missing something.

We have to remember: not only are we innately selfish, serving our own interests over others, but we cannot see the whole picture. And the missing piece may be the one thing that makes sense of all the rest. James had to learn this lesson the hard way, just as Myles had to learn his own lesson of humility.

Being truly sorry demanded change in us. Only those around us can really say whether that change has been real. We certainly hope so.

Think of what or who might need your forgiveness in your own life. Remember that unforgiveness is a chain around your own neck. And yet, your freedom from the weight of it lies within the power of your own will.

In his book, *Total Forgiveness*, the writer RT Kendall reminds us that forgiveness is not approving.

It's not approving of what was done; it's not excusing or justifying the offending act. It's not pretending you were never hurt. It's not a kind of blindness to what was done. It's not forgetting or simply making up and carrying on while ignoring the hurt caused between you and the offender.

Rather, it is an act of the will. It acknowledges the hurt. It does not gloss over it. But it also acknowledges that we are both selfish people, and the only way selfish people can build friendships, marriages, families, communities, nations and cultures, is to be prepared to say sorry and to forgive.

Forgiveness is the only real foundation on which to build a culture of genuine peace and tolerance. As Nelson Mandela clearly understood.

Time does not heal. It's what you do with that time that heals.

Be sorry. Turn Around. Make a change. Walk away.

Make a choice. Don't be a victim. Forgive.

Chapter Four

CONNECT & ABANDON

James was standing next to an older man the other day who said to him, 'I think I'm going to shoot the next person who tells me that they're on a "personal journey."'

Funnily enough, he did own a shotgun, but he didn't strike James as the sort of man who was open to learning many new lessons in life so perhaps his attitude wasn't surprising.

And while the notion that life is a journey may indeed be a cliché, that's only because it corresponds pretty well with how most of us actually experience life. We progress in time and space; we change; circumstances around us change, too, like the scenery passing us by.

But if we concede that life is something like a journey, then immediately the question arises: what's our destination? Where are we going? Are we heading in a particular direction or just cruising through the landscape with no particular objective in mind?

This chapter looks at purpose. It also looks at how knowing or choosing that purpose affects our relationships, in particular our friendships. We want to explore how best to manage and interact with the other travellers and visitors, the people who come and go in our life.

*

God & Purpose

If you're going on a journey you might jump into your car or your van, and one of the first things you're likely to do is punch your destination into your Sat-Nav. Within moments, it has calculated the most efficient way of getting to where you want to go. You set off following its instructions. So far so good. But maybe along the way you take a wrong turn, or you hit heavy traffic. Maybe the car breaks down. Maybe you get stuck on a roundabout going round and round, and keep missing your exit. Whatever might go wrong, the Sat-Nav is always able to recalculate the best route onwards rather than sending you back the way you came.

We think of God a bit like that. He is the Author of human purpose. But at the same time, He is also the all-knowing computer and the destination. What He says and thinks and expects of us is therefore helpful to know. In a very real sense, we believe God defines our true purpose.

We don't want to go into the idea of God much more than that within these pages. But it would be disingenuous of us if we didn't mention God.

So there He is...and there He will continue to be.

So what if you're not sure where you're going?

You may well ask yourself: Is there a bigger purpose to my life? Is there a destination? Is there a God?

Does He care what I do with my life? Is there more to life than what I can immediately see and touch and feel in front of me?

These are not small questions.

Even so, we think the Authentic Man should have an answer to them. And if he doesn't yet, then he should certainly spend some time reflecting on them until he sees more, however vague and ill-defined those revelations may be.

However, since this isn't a theology book, this is not the place to tackle those questions head on. (Though if you are up for asking those kinds of questions, we recommend trying an Alpha Course. There's info about how in Appendix C.)

In any case, whether you feel you have a clear purpose for your life, whether you believe in a higher power, actually being on the journey itself is inescapable. You just can't avoid it.

And what we all discover pretty quickly is that other people have come along for the ride.

*

My Guys
As you journey onward in life, there will be a whole load of people with you along the way. Parents, siblings, a select few lifelong friends. Others you pick up as you go along (your partner, for example; children maybe). Some are in for the long haul; others stay a while and then split off again. Some you leave trailing behind you; others stretch away ahead of you.

How we navigate the flux of these changing relationships is crucial. How we connect well, but how we abandon well, too. How we hold on and move on. That is what we want to talk about in this chapter.

*

No Man Is An Island
Independence sounds like a good thing. That feels true whether we're talking about a nation or a man. It's important to 'be your own man;' to 'stand on your own two feet;' 'to forge your own path.' Or so we think.

But the reality is that humans don't do well when they are truly cut off from others. We hope it's been implicit throughout this book, but now we are saying it directly: humans are born to have connection with each other. That is true whether you are an introvert who prefers their own company or a massive extrovert who constantly wants to be around other people. Humans are relational beasts – even though, as men, we tend to downplay this side of our humanity.

Psychologists say that we are in a friendship recession right now. People – not just men – feel more disconnected than ever, in spite of the appearance of connection on social media in particular. Directly related to this, male suicide rates are increasing – a reflection of all the loneliness. A recent study showed that the two most common self-descriptors of suicidal men are 'useless' and 'worthless.' This makes some sense, since if you don't appreciate your worth or value, then you are unlikely to know your use in this world.

Often the way we get our value is to be needed and known by others around us.

That means friendship. That means connection.

*

Friendship Through Experience

It's ironic that most of our friendships are based purely on coincidence. Interactions with others often occur by chance and not the result of our own choosing. We meet our school friends in a school that our parents chose or else we went to because it was located in an area where we happened to grow up. The same is true if you go to university. Then the same with work friends. For most of us, there's a tendency to think of friendships in quite a passive way – they sort of happen to form around us in an organic way. Of course, often this works well. But we think that men should be as intentional about their friendships as they are in all other areas of their life. You can choose your friendships.

The Authentic Man makes no excuses for this.

There comes a point in life when most men have the sense to get up off their butt out of their neighbourhood, cross the river, go hang out with some different groups, not only the ones they happened to grow up amongst. It's not hard. We make it sound hard. But all it requires is a bit of initiative.

If you cling to the same few friends you happened to go to school with, you are making a big choice when it comes to your purpose and the direction your life will take. Motivational speaker Jim Rohn asserts that you will inevitably become the average of the five people you hang out with the most. Therefore, if that's the same blokes you grew up with, then that will be your ceiling. But if you want more for yourself, if you want a more expansive life, then you need to be intentional – even strategic – about the group of people you choose to spend time with.

Responsibility

And no – this is not about finding a way into the 'in-crowd.' Rather, it's about being true to yourself and to your purpose – as far as you can tell what that is. If you feel within yourself that you need to grow, to expand your world, then don't let the friendships you have put a limit on that. You should move as your growth demands. (And this is actually one of the best life hacks a young man can do. Leave home. Move to a new city. Make new friends.)

*

Connect...
Of course, the seasons of life will and do affect friendships profoundly. A man's twenties especially are a period of change, of exploration and discovery. So if you're reading this book and you're in your twenties, the chances are there are probably a lot of other men who feel the same way, who are looking for different friends too. Maybe they moved to a new town. Maybe they've launched into a new career. They have aspirations for their life, and they are looking to find the new adult friendships which will form around those aspirations, and ideally strengthen them. So be open to making new connections. Invest time in building friendships that make sense of the next visible stretch of road that you can see for your life.

A friend of ours called Phil describes his own experience of feeling cut off, sitting alone on the sofa at home waiting for other people to call him, and suddenly realising that he must be far from unique. Many other men are doing just the same. Unfortunately these days sitting at home with a phone in hand, it may feel like we are doing something, feel like we are connected, when the reality is we are sitting in a room alone and achieving very little. Phil's solution to the problem is borrowed from a German friend. The phrase is, *'Machen Sie Spaß.'* It translates, 'Make your own fun.' Phil was amused that this played into one stereotype of the Germans: that they are always very organised about everything. He wasn't surprised that their approach to friendship falls in the same vein: they organise their own fun. What this actually means is that they are proactive about making friends and about having fun within those friendships. About creating experiences. Without that level of proactivity, men reach an age where fun doesn't just happen spontaneously. It requires effort, which may be why male friendship is in decline.

The progress of life does not help this, as people you were once close to meet partners, get married, have kids, move away, buy homes, build businesses and so on. All of that reduces the time available for friendship.

Again, men have to get off their butts if they want to invest in and maintain life-giving and life-affirming friendships. Friendships that will give them that value and purpose of which we spoke earlier.

*

...and Abandon
But in order to make new connections, you need the space in your life to do so. Which means as well as being able to connect, you also need to be able to abandon. By that, we mean move on. Sometimes the abandonment part of the journey can stir up a lot of difficult emotions. Especially if you feel like the abandoned one, rather than the one doing the abandoning. Again, think moving on.

As we've explained, some friendships run their course. Lives, particularly of friends, that run in parallel for a very long time are actually quite rare. More often, one of you reaches a fork in the road, and the distance between you grows wider, until you can no longer feel them beside you. You never hear from them; you never meet up anymore. It can feel like a loss. Even like a betrayal. But letting go of a friendship is an important part of moving on in life, particularly as your own purpose becomes clearer.

We may well grieve a friendship, but so long as we don't stay in the place of grieving for too long, we can also see it as an opportunity. We now have space for new friendships. The trick is being intentional about connecting with someone else – and also not leaving it too long before we do so. If not, we are likely only ever to experience abandonment. And because everyone's journey is so specific to them, this means that we're likely to find ourselves alone before we've gotten very far.

Not a good place to be, as we have said.

*

Identify Your Friendships
As you leave some friendships behind and encounter new people with whom to form new friendships, it's helpful to understand that there are different kinds of friendship, and to be able to identify which friends fall into which category.

The Greek philosopher Aristotle spoke of three different types of friendship. We think his model is helpful for making sense of our network of connections, and how our own interaction could and should adapt, depending on the type of each friendship.

Aristotle's first type is a friendship of *utility*. These friendships are with people from whom you extract value. This may sound a bit mercenary, but in essence they are based on what two people can do for one another. Maybe they shout you a pint down the pub in return for a ride home. Maybe your kids go to the same school and you do play dates. Maybe you work in the same team at the office, and the other guy can make you look good in front of your boss. Maybe you're locked up in jail, and he can scrounge stuff you need. The friendship falls away the moment you no longer have any use for the other.

Aristotle's second type is a friendship of *pleasure*. These are friendships based on a shared activity and the pursuit of fleeting pleasures or emotions. Maybe you support the same football club. Maybe you play golf together. Maybe you lift weights together. Maybe you both like to go clubbing, or go to the same parties. It's the guy you would happily drink with but never have over for a BBQ. These friendships can be short-lived as well. As soon as one of you loses interest in the shared activity, the friendship is unlikely to last.

In both these cases, whilst the connection is often genuine and helpful, ultimately the other person is not being valued as a friend for who they are, but rather for what they have or what they do.

The third type of friendship which Aristotle identifies is a friendship of *virtue*. This he considers to be true friendship. These are with people you like for themselves, the people who push you to be a better person. The underlying motivation is that you actually care about this person, and therefore the friendship is likely to be much more stable and outlast any changes in circumstances or interests. These are the hardest friendships to find, perhaps because they are the ones of greatest value. You need to invest time to create a friendship of virtue.

Of course, although the last type has the most value, it's not a bad thing to have a variety of the other two types as well. In fact, it's probably inevitable. But you shouldn't be surprised that, when circumstances change or their interests and enthusiasms change, those friendships fall away. When this happens, you can look around for other people to fill those gaps.

Another way of looking at friendships, devised by anthropologist Robin Dunbar, suggests that any individual only has a capacity for five high quality and intimate friendships. These are the people who will be there for you whatever joys or disasters befall you, through sickness and strife, and into old age. You can share anything with them.

The next level of intimacy, he asserts, supports between twelve and fifteen friends. These are your good friends, with whom you might regularly meet up for a coffee and a chat.

The next level out are your general pool of friends, numbering around fifty. These are people you might catch up with from time to time, and when any one of them has a birthday party, say, or some special occasion you'll probably see many of them there. But you're unlikely to see each individual regularly. They are more like a mixture of the friends of utility and pleasure, as Aristotle defines them.

According to Dunbar, the outermost circle of

intimacy are people you know – more like friendly acquaintances – but rarely see, and rarely actively make an effort to see. These number around a hundred and fifty.

Dunbar's figures tend to include family connections as well. So you can quickly see why you are unlikely to have more than one or two true blood-brother friends with whom you can share anything and everything.

The trick is knowing where our friends sit and relating to them at each level of intimacy in an appropriate way, especially in terms of what you share with them.

But try applying it. You'll soon figure out if you've got it wrong.

Myles was recently on holiday in the Lake District with his family. He just got back to the cottage after a run, and he stopped outside to do a little stretching before heading back in. It was early and the kids were not up yet. He just had time to shower and be ready for the day.

As he was stretching out his calf muscles, a woman opened the upper window of a neighbouring cottage and called down.

'Lovely morning, isn't it?'
'Oh yeah, lovely, beautiful,' returned Myles politely, already thinking it was a bit early for neighbourly chit-chat.
'Been for a run then?'
'Yes, round the lake and back. Stunning.'
Pause. 'I can't run. I had an operation.'
'Oh...ah ...Sorry about that.'

Responsibility

'Mmm.' *Pause*. 'My husband died, you know.'
'Oh wow. Oh dear.' Myles now has no idea what to say. This is getting weird. He starts edging towards the back door.
'He built this house.'
'Oh.'
Long pause. 'He looked like Tom Cruise. Ever so handsome.'
'Oh lovely.'
Pause. 'Yeah...' *Sigh*. 'He died at work. Fell off his ladder. They called an ambulance, but it didn't get there in time.'
'Oh dear.'
'That was fifteen years ago.' At this point, she starts crying. 'Fifteen years.'
'...Erm...I'm going to go. Gotta get my kids up.'
Wiping eyes. 'I've got kids. Down in London. They're grown up. Both directors of their own companies, you know.'
'Oh. That's great. Erm...'

It's not clear exactly when or how Myles managed to extricate himself from this conversation, only that this woman had absolutely no sense of appropriate boundaries. She was clearly struggling with multiple things, and Myles did feel some sympathy for her.

Perhaps you're the sort of bloke who would have stayed chatting for hours with her, but Myles left only feeling the awkwardness of the encounter. The following morning he did his stretching inside the house.

Within each friendship, evaluate what is and isn't appropriate to share. In case you are in any doubt, it's completely inappropriate to share your life story with a total stranger over a boundary fence at six in the morning.

Of course, while oversharing is bad, that is rarely men's problem. Far more likely, we wouldn't give up even that level of detail to our best friend. Once more, we strike upon that idea of **balance**. You don't want to be the guy who overshares with your friends – that becomes boring and often awkward. But nor do you want to share absolutely nothing of yourself. Especially when things get rough.

For those who do, this can have tragic consequences.

A recent study by the Samaritans charity revealed that suicide is the number one cause of death for men under forty-five in the UK and male suicide rates are more than three times higher than females. We know many stories of guys who have taken their own lives and many families who have experienced the agony of this.

Three years ago, a friend of James took his own life. He had gotten into financial difficulties and became completely overwhelmed by the situation he was in. James had no idea this was going on, and when speaking to other friends at the man's funeral, that seemed to be the common theme amongst them. None of even his closest friends knew of his financial woes that were causing him such existential agony. The real tragedy is that, by the standards of most people, the financial hole he was in was not that deep. It just felt that way to him. He could see no way out. But because he never revealed any of this to his friends, they had no opportunity to do anything about it. Neither to offer him counsel and comfort, nor to offer any practical financial support.

If only the man had been willing to share his vulnerabilities as well as his strengths to his closest friends, perhaps he would still be alive. Instead, he chose a tragically permanent solution to what could have been only a temporary problem.

We want to be really clear. If you are entertaining suicidal thoughts, please reach out to someone close to you and tell them about it. If you don't feel you have anyone who could listen, in Appendix B we steer you towards some professional programmes which help counsel people through difficult times, including spiralling debt. Whatever you do, don't suffer those thoughts in silence, no matter the problems underlying them.

In short, be intentional about your friendships.

Part of that means being able to identify the nature of a particular friendship, as we have said. Is it a friendship of virtue – one which is based on your appreciation of the other person for who they are. Or is it more distant? A friendship of pleasure or utility? In which case, learn to adjust your reliance on and expectation of that friend accordingly. The reality is, as men, we don't always care when someone not that close to us shares something that is obviously important to them. We know that for ourselves, so be aware of that in others.

If you are unsure about a particular friendship, often it is the tough times that reveal our truest friends. It's only when the night is darkest that we can see the stars to navigate by. For those other friendships, it's okay to let them go when they've had their time. To abandon, to move on. So long as your circle of friends does not deplete to nothing. And always keep an eye out for new friendships which might replace the old.

Connect. Abandon. Connect again.

*

Gangs

As men, we tend to be much more gang oriented than women. Traditionally, up and down the social scale, there have always been groups of men – from the gentlemen's club of St James', London, to the working men's club of pretty much any town up and down the country. These clubs spawn in many different directions. Almost any area of interest will generate a club. Sports clubs, hobby clubs, arts clubs, walking clubs, youth clubs, street gangs and now even communities like Men's Shed.

The psychologist and author Jordan Peterson asserts that the question is not whether young men will become a member of a gang. Rather, what kind of a gang will it be?

Even the word 'gang' tends to carry negative connotations, associated as it is with crime and violence. But what draws us into even the wrong kind of gang is the healthy desire to belong. This need to belong is not just a male trait but a very human need, and is probably biologically hard-wired into us from millennia into our distant past. In that more physically dangerous world, the need to be an accepted member of a tribe was key to an individual's survival. Being ostracised from your tribe meant almost certain death. No wonder it remains such a powerful driver within us all today.

The challenge then for men is how to build healthy connections of belonging. It's a natural inclination within most of us to want to be around other men. The instinct for men to collaborate towards some

Responsibility

greater goal, to be part of a pack, is very strong, and often rewarding. Personally, we have never felt so brave as when surrounded by lots of other men cheering us on, encouraging us, driving us in the same direction. One easily imagines this, thinking of football or cricket teams, crews on a ship, companies in an army. The sense of belonging between a group of men can be a beautiful thing, empowering and enriching to the individual, calling them to a better, bolder version of themselves. A true band of brothers.

What kind of a gang are you a part of right now? Is the culture of that gang calling you to a better or a worse version of yourself? Be honest.

Remember, there's no honour among thieves.

Are you hanging with a bunch of guys who simply facilitate your most destructive behaviours? Maybe it's stealing or gambling; maybe it's casual violence or casual sex; maybe it's drinking or drug addiction. If it's not good for you or not good for other people, get out.

Friends who object or ridicule you the moment you take a step towards cleaning yourself up were never any friends of yours in the first place. Make a note of them, and do what is necessary to disconnect from them.

On the other hand, those friends with whom you can share bad news without drawing their judgement, as much as good news without drawing their jealousy – those are good friends worth investing your time in. Make a note of them too.

And don't forget: *Machen sie Spaß*.

*

Stuck On The Roundabout
Here again, we run into the theme of addiction. To return to our journey analogy – various kinds of addictions or compulsions are a bit like being stuck on a roundabout, going round and round and never able to move forward, because you're unable to find the right exit.

You may know men like this. You may be one yourself.

You're able to identify them because their life feels like a series of repeating cycles. Affair after affair; marriage after marriage. The same patterns of failure repeating over and over again. You're looking for the next high; the next drink; the next vacation; the next deal; the next shiny new gadget. But somehow you're not growing as a human being, not maturing as a man, not progressing towards some ultimate purpose. In the end, it is an exhausting and frustrating way to live.

If this is you, if you feel trapped in a repeating cycle of addiction, seek out professional help. One of the steps on the 12-step programme to help alcoholics and addicts find freedom is to change 'people, places, and things.'

That friend that always has a little coke in his wallet. That club where you always seem to make poor life choices that you regret in the morning. That website that always seems to call to you late at night when you're feeling lonely and have had a drink. These can all have a power over you which is hard, if not impossible, to break on your own. But you can take the first step towards finding an exit and moving on with your life. Seek help. Call a friend who cares. Speak to someone. (Again, we've put the details of several organisations we recommend who can help in Appendix B.)

Without this, you become just another man who never grew up.

James has a friend who is now well into his forties. He's never managed to form a relationship with a partner that lasts longer than a few months. And yet, in some ways, he's a romantic. He has convinced himself he goes out on the dating scene looking for love. In fact, all he really finds is sex. Great, you might think – but as we've said, even the greatest Don Juan discovers sooner or later that, ultimately, sex on its own – even a lot of it – doesn't make for a very fulfilling life. When James met up with this guy recently, his friend said he was looking for a partner again, but at least he realised it was only going to work with a woman who was slightly older than the women he normally dated. He was now seeking someone in their late thirties or early forties. When James asked him where he was looking, he named various nightclubs around the city. 'So you want to meet a single woman in her forties who's out clubbing in those sorts of places?' James asked pointedly.

'Describe what she's like, this woman.' The guy didn't have an answer. Confronted with the contradiction between what he really wanted and the way he was going about getting it, he suddenly recognised how stuck he was.

Sometimes you have to abandon what is familiar to you if you're going to create space to connect with something better. Something real and lasting and fulfilling.

*

New Friends
Another way of expanding your connections – and so your world – is to try doing something you've never done before. This also has the added bonus of connecting you to people you wouldn't normally meet. We think this is very good for the Authentic Man, too.

Have you ever stretched to something entirely new, something way outside your comfort zone? How did it go? Who were the people involved? Did it change them? Did it change you?

Unlikely as it sounds, Myles once had a try-out as a Morris dancer. For the uninitiated, Morris dancing is an archaic form of English folk dance. Yes – it's the guys you sometimes see prancing around market squares, dressed all in white, with bells and ribbons and sticks that go clackety-clack. Perhaps like Myles, you thought there was something vaguely comic about this activity, if not that the blokes doing it must surely be weirdos.

One day in summer, he happened to be walking along the Brighton seafront with a friend when they came across a Morris dancing troop. At first they were amused and exchanged the usual disparaging comments about how embarrassing it is that this is the English national dance. (Compared to, say, the New Zealand Haka.) But after a while Myles realised the men actually doing the dancing didn't look embarrassed at all. On the contrary, they looked like they were having a great time. Eventually Myles turned to his friend. 'You know what, I think these guys are having good craic.' He was so struck by them that he approached one dancer after their performance for a chat. They swapped details and the Morris dancer said he'd to be in touch. His name was Derek. He came across as a sound bloke. But even then, Myles assumed Derek must be the 'normal' one who organised all the other weirdos. It was actually a few months later when Derek texted Myles asking him if he would like to come to practice.

Somewhat doubtful, Myles agreed, but decide to take along some back-up in case he got kidnapped or something equally unexpected. But he and his friends Caleb and Noa soon discovered a community of men that totally took them by surprise.

The venue turned out to be a little village hall, full of about forty men. When they tentatively stuck their heads round the door, everyone stopped thwacking their sticks and came say to hello and shake their hands. They asked questions; they introduced themselves. Then Myles and friends were split off into a group to learn a routine.

He found the dancing was actually quite fun, much more so than he expected. At the end of the evening Myles and his friends had to perform for the rest of the group. Caleb was particularly good and the men were suitably enthusiastic about their latest recruits.

After dancing, a trip to the pub was mandatory. But rather than the usual awkward queuing at the bar, with these guys you just sat down and it was all on the house. There was a rule that each time they performed and got paid, the money went straight into the communal bar kitty, so they spent the money hanging out together. Myles asked a few different guys why they joined, and what kept them in. Most said they were looking for friends. Looking for connection. He heard stories of members helping each other through tough financial times, through poor mental health, through loneliness, offering each other a kind of family away from home. They were men of all ages, anywhere from twenty-five to seventy, with the natural flow of wisdom that these kinds of inter-generational friendships can bring.

Myles had never seen anything like it.

Of course, their new Morris dancing buddies were very keen that Myles and Caleb should sign up as permanent members. Which was flattering. But they weren't quite ready to become fully paid-up Morris dancers just yet.

What James loves about that story is that when they first saw the group out dancing, most men would have remained in that posture of sceptical observer: thinking that Morris dancing was weird and embarrassing for performers and spectators alike. But Myles was brave enough to approach them and say he was willing to give it a go. Sometimes you have to say something out loud to be witness to your own commitment.

Myles was good as his word. The club followed up with him. Connection was sought; connection was offered. The welcome was warm. The laughter was free. The beer never ran dry.

*

Work It Out
So, knowing where we're headed, even in the

vaguest terms, helps us make sense of who and what we should connect with and when. And, at least as important, who and what we should abandon when it inhibits us from progressing onward towards the ultimate purpose of our lives.

God, guys and gangs – all of these will shape us. Being intentional about how and why we need to connect with each of them, in a positive and fruitful way, will help us find our path in life, whatever obstacles the journey throws down before us.

Connect. Abandon. Connect again.

Chapter Five

FUN & HEALTHY

You may be wondering when we're going to run out of advice for you. Here's the good news. There are not many chapters left, and this one is short.

The reason we've kept it short is that we think much of the stuff we are going to discuss is so obvious and has been covered in so many other places by authors and experts far more qualified than us that there is not a lot that we want to add. However, having said that...if we *didn't* mention anything about pursuing a fun and healthy lifestyle, it would leave a big hole in the picture of what it means to be the Authentic Man.

Essentially, what we are trying to say is that the Authentic Man is able to keep things light-hearted, he knows how to have a good time, but at the same time he keeps himself in good shape, so that he will be able to enjoy that good time for the rest of his life and play an active part in it.

Food, drink, exercise, pastimes, passions and hobbies – these are the areas we will cover in brief. But while we want to offer some common-sense advice, we don't want to be too directive about the detail. As for several chapters of this book, the thread that runs through this chapter is *balance*. Operating out in the extremes tends to create more problems than it solves, as we'll explain.

But first, a short story.

Myles was in Aldi the other day, where he usually buys nuts and seeds and occasionally the odd fillet steak. He found himself in line behind a father of two sons who were running riot, totally out of control. The dad was probably in his thirties. Big guy, substantial belly, and slow on his feet as a result. Tough looking though. When his boys of about four and six wouldn't do as they were told, he tried to catch them. But he was simply too slow and the six-year-old especially knew it. It became embarrassing. When it was his turn to get his groceries scanned, his pile was backing up the conveyor belt because his kids had run off and he was busy chasing them while they ran rings around him. They weren't really being naughty, just being kids.

Myles felt sorry for the guy. Maybe he had some health issues, but on the whole for most men in that state it is self-induced. Myles wondered what was a reasonable age for a man's kids to be able to outrun him. Probably not his thirties. In any case, if there is any messaging out there for men to live a healthy and balanced lifestyle, this guy clearly hadn't got the memo. Myles couldn't help thinking that to let yourself get in that physical state couldn't be much fun for the kids either. This guy was more like a grandad to them already. They must be missing out on so much, Myles thought.

Our physical well-being as men is what we're going to think about now.

Of course, we understand there is a wide spectrum of physicality to consider. And to be clear from the outset, we are not advocating that men should be ripped to the core – or that when you take your shirt off you should look like that guy on the cover of Men's Health magazine. In fact, research shows that the only people who notice how 'jacked' a man is are other men.

James tested this theory the other day. He found himself next to a guy in the sauna at his local gym. This bloke had a great physique. James and he got chatting and James asked him whether women ever commented on his toned body. His answer was, 'Never!' In his experience, whether he was in the gym or on the beach or wherever, it was only ever men who complimented him, even though he used to be a model. But women were just not interested in how muscular or ripped he was. In fact, he said, they thought that if anything his body signalled that he was too vain. They seemed much more interested in what kind of a man he was rather than what he looked like. It's certainly something to bear in mind if you're spending all your spare time in the gym. You're really only going to impress other men.

Obviously these two examples represent two physical extremes. And what we don't want to do is give anyone a complex about what they should look like. Rather, what we are suggesting is that in the area of your physical well-being, keep it **fun** and **healthy**.

*

Fun & Healthy - What Does That Look Like?
In general terms, we think men should be healthy enough to live an active life. So what is that? Well, you should be able to do a few press-ups. You should be able to lift/chin-up your own bodyweight (at least once – think climbing over a wall). You should be able to go for a run; to walk up a flight of stairs without being out of breath. Simple stuff, not excessive, but some basic indicators that your body is in reasonable shape.

In a sense, the two of us represent two quite

different approaches to our physical well-being. Myles is much more obsessed with exercise. He finds it baffling that anyone would not want to exercise every day. He gets itchy and restless when he hasn't exercised during the day. And it's not unknown for him to break out in a few lunges in the middle of a conversation with him, just to get the muscles working. In fact, no joke – he has just done 15 press-ups on the kitchen floor, because he was getting bored of writing this book. He is much more conscious of what he eats than James; much more disciplined and deliberate about what he puts into his own body. (For example, James had six cookies at lunch today. Myles had none.)

James, by contrast, is completely uninterested in establishing any regular disciplined exercise routine. In general, he'll avoid or put off exercise unless it's for fun or else serves some other purpose (as we'll come onto in a moment). He is fortunate that his wife, Emiko, has taught him how to eat properly, or at least to know the difference between good eating and bad.

Neither of us are in incredible shape. Neither of us are serious athletes. If Myles took his shirt off, you might be mildly impressed. If James took his shirt off, you might see a hint of 'moobs.' But sport and physical activity is definitely part of our connection as friends. We've done a lot of things together, especially the XCC weekends, which we've run together many times. As we explained in the introduction, these are mind, body and soul adventures, specifically for men, which span a few days in very remote places. Physically, they are demanding, involving very long walks over challenging terrain in hard and arduous conditions. We've been on these time and time again, because we think it's important for men to be active and to stretch themselves. For men to find their limits, and then see that in fact they can push beyond those limits with a little determination. Whenever we've been on holiday together, there's usually something active involved. Physical activity has been a big theme for us and our friendship, and so we feel it's important to offer that to other men as well.

You might find that a jarring contrast – at least in James. That he's not really interested in exercise regimes but is still regularly involved in something as physical as the XCC weekends that he runs. But for him, there's no contradiction. He sees his body as a tool, as a resource for him to move around those landscapes that are also good for his mind and his soul. He sees physical resilience as being linked to any kind of resilience. Physical strength is linked to any kind of strength. In that sense, finding your physical limits and pushing them a little further Is not only about your physical capacity; it's about increasing your mental and emotional capacity, too.

The capacity of your will as a man.

He feels that his body should reflect what is going on inside of him. If you can't get to these remote wilderness places because your body won't allow it, that's not a good sign. Those places are challenging but they are not beyond the capacity of most men.

Equally, if the body and physical fitness and strength become too much the focus, that's not a good thing either. The fitness model at James' gym admitted he was actually quite miserable a lot of the time. The health regime he maintained was so rigorous, so disciplined, so restrictive, that he rarely went out. He had to say no to most things and most social occasions, because they were incompatible with his dietary demands or training routine.

The two of us have struggled with this a bit in our friendship. Quite often, out for an evening or on holiday, Myles would have had a couple of drinks and then decide he was ready to call it a night by 10pm when, as far as James was concerned, the night was just getting started. But we usually find a balance, especially if we are getting up to do something active the next morning.

*

Find Your Balance
The idea of balance is an important one, as we've said.

It's a no-brainer that no one really wants to be out on the unhealthy extreme. But at the other extreme, being too health conscious, too obsessed with exercise, too enthusiastic about whatever happens to be your hobby or your passion creates a whole other set of problems as well.

Jack Ma, the Chinese billionaire and co-founder of Alibaba, said that his advice to his son when it came to his schooling was that the best place to be in any class was somewhere in the middle. The students who consistently come top of the class tend to feel the pressure to follow a similar well-trodden path for high achievers through the rest of their life, trying to be top of everything. And obviously you don't want to be languishing at the bottom. So Ma's view is that being in the middle and maintaining and developing a healthy range of interests outside of your immediate academic studies would give you career options later in life that would never occur to you while you are growing up and progressing through your schooling and help keep a good life balance.

We think you can transfer this advice to other areas of life, too. Unless you're on course to be a serious professional athlete, you don't want to be the fittest person you know or the one most obsessed with sport, stuck prioritising sustained activity over connection. Nor do you want to be the top shagger; they may draw some misplaced admiration from their peer group for a while, but often they end up the middle-aged bachelor, sad and lonely, while the rest of their friends have figured out how to have a sustainable relationship. You don't want to be the funniest in a group, because then it falls to you to always be up, always be the one entertaining. Or the richest in a group, always feeling the pressure to pay for others; or the poorest in the group, always feeling you can't afford to keep up with your friends or else leaning too hard on their generosity.

It may sound old-fashioned, but we think the key to staying fun and healthy is to take everything in moderation. As a general rule, it seems pretty wise. A man who lives by the motto, 'Everything in moderation,' will usually fare pretty well in life.

*

Passions & Pastimes
Of course we are all different. We are into different things. Some interests become passions. Some passions become obsessions.

So it's always worth checking yourself to see how your passions fit in with the rest of your life.

A pastime that eats up all your time and energy and

money may be fine for *you*, but what about the people around you? What about your partner or your family?

Think about the weekend warriors. You know the type: driven guys who work extreme hours during the week, and at the weekend they turn into Triathlon Man or Marathon Man or Football Man or Golfing Man or Motorbike Man. Often they used to be athletes in their youth, and they train as if they're still on track for an Olympic medal. But they're really not. We heard of one who would disappear for three or four hours every Saturday morning to go cycling.

And when he returned he was so shattered from the morning's exercise and had pushed himself so hard that he needed to sleep for another two hours afterwards. Meanwhile his wife was struggling to look after three kids under ten. Is it any wonder her head was turned one lonely Saturday by another man who seemed more engaged with his own fathering? No one cares that you've done an Iron-Man if that makes you an absentee father or husband. Your kids care more about your quality time with them, than the time of your new PB. They just want to be with their dad.

So be honest with yourself. How much time are you spending on your hobbies? What is the impact of this on those around you? Are they comfortable with it? Have you talked it through with them to see what they think?

Then consider how much money do you spend on your hobby?

Men love kit, we all know that. Whether it's cycling, motorbikes, cars, golf, fishing, surfing, or whatever else – all these activities demand a lot of kit. Much of it, expensive. Be honest with how much it costs. In our experience, the spend on these things is higher than people think. And most often, it's hidden and un-negotiated from those others in your life.

So whether it's sport or some other pastime, if it's not your actual profession, we suggest that your pursuit of it should leave you more energised and alive and engaged rather than exhausted or over-burdened. And it shouldn't be causing any undue tension, distress or burden to those around you.

For some of you, you need the competitive edge in your life. You love the fight, you love the contest. We get that. You want to beat your PB; you want to beat your mate on Peloton; you want to beat someone at...whatever. It's a necessary part of who you are. But even you should be able to find the right balance between extremes, so that it has a positive effect on your life as a whole.

At the other end of the spectrum are those who struggle to do anything active at all.

These are the guys whose plan for the weekend is nothing but downtime and screen-time. At best, they might go out to watch others play sport and drink a few beers, or maybe catch a film or an exhibition. But if they get the chance to spend the weekend in their onesie – or never get out of their pyjamas at all – they're happy. The problem here isn't that they are resting – appropriate amounts of downtime is good for us all – or that they follow sport or enjoy a beer with their mates. The problem is the passive and inactive lifestyle. While the weekend warrior is out on his bike miles away, these guys are at home, but they're off in a different world altogether. Is that you? Does this sound familiar?

Are your kids begging you to take them to the park, while you're stuck on trying to complete Level 14 of the latest video game, or you're deep into season three of the latest Netflix series?

The problem isn't Netflix; the problem isn't your PlayStation. The problem is you being absent from your responsibilities for too long, too often.

We will all have a lot of different motives for doing a lot of different things: some conscious, some unconscious; some good, some bad. But at a very basic level, asking ourselves, 'Is it still fun? Is it healthy? Am I giving it the right amount of time?' seems to us like a good way to stay more or less in balance.

*

Food & Drink & Everything Else
You don't have to be a dietary expert or aware of the latest food fads to look at yourself in the mirror, and if your belly is significantly overhanging your waistband, realise that it's time to lose a few kilos. That it's time to eat less and move more.

For most of us, this is a reasonable demand. If, for some, even this is not enough or too hard, then it may be necessary to seek specialist help to return to a healthy balance in life. But likely you already knew that.

Less food, less sugar, less booze, less smoking. Drugs...again, less.

It's all pretty obvious, right? We don't really need to

spell it all out.

By far the greatest cost burden on the NHS is treating patients suffering from diseases caused by lifestyle choices. Smoking, alcohol, drugs, high salt, high cholesterol and high sugar diets all leave us vulnerable to some pretty nasty consequences, which ultimately won't just be your problem to deal with. The longer it goes on the more that others are going to have to support you. So, making only a few small but significant changes now will mean you'll be able to enjoy life a lot more and for a lot longer than you otherwise would. And that others will be able to enjoy you for longer, too.

*

Addiction Again
We have heard the stories of countless men whose lives have been wrecked by alcohol. Not only the toll it takes on your physical body, but the situations it places you in, the state of mind it creates in you. Men do things under the influence of alcohol that they would not dream of doing when they're sober. But too often their actions have serious, sometimes fatal, consequences, both for themselves and for others. We all know that having one drink and then another can be fun for a while, but each of us has a different point at which something flips. Do you have a handle on when that limit is reached? Are you able to pull back and retain control of yourself? If not, you should consider rethinking your drinking habits.

A couple we know are the most doting parents. They give their children absolutely everything they can and adore them to bits. And yet they seem to have one glaring blind spot. (One of those gorillas we mentioned in Chapter Two, remember?) They think it's okay to get really drunk around their kids. One of them in particular often becomes quite volatile and aggressive. It frightens their children in a direct sense (they feel threatened), but indirectly, they also get very anxious seeing their parents in that state. It makes them feel insecure, especially within their home in the evening time, when they need to feel safest.

Let's be explicit about this. If you can't remember what happened last night, then you've drunk too much. You need to rein it in. If you struggle to rein it in, then do something about it – like, give away some of your drinking money to a charity so that you have less to spend on alcohol. If that doesn't work, then seek out other help. (Alcoholics Anonymous, for example, again, see notes in Appendix B.)

Taking it a step further, let's talk about drugs. We both know a few people who think that drugs and alcohol are interchangeable in terms of what they offer and deliver. However, we know absolutely no one who regularly takes drugs who ends up happy in the long term. Seriously. No one. Ever.

In fact, in our opinion and experience, it's the total opposite. So, the challenge to you is this: are you sure you have your drug use under control? Or are drugs controlling you? Can you contradict what we've just said?

To be totally frank, the Authentic Men we know don't take drugs. So there is your challenge.

Again, if you're struggling in this area, we recommend the Narcotics Anonymous (NA) programme. We have seen countless lives transformed through this course.

Similarly for porn. There is basically no healthy reason for regularly looking at porn. As an industry, it represents one of the darkest corners of humanity, involving sex trafficking and the exploitation of children all over the world. According to the International Centre for Missing and Exploited Children, well over 100,000 children go missing in the UK every year. In the US, this figure is closer to half a million. Many of these poor kids end up falling into the hands of those who profit from the sex industry. None of us should be putting money in the hands of people like that if we can avoid it.

But even for us men personally, porn is corrosive for the mind, for the body and for the most significant relationships in our lives. We've heard the stories of so many men who dabble in it for fun, and slowly but surely it sinks its claws deeper and deeper into their lives until they can't stop even when they want to. Porn seems like harmless fun, but it has the power to destroy everything you are trying to build. There's not much to say about it other than *stop it now*. If you can't stop it, seek help.

As for food...Food is of course a good thing, but it's also clear that even food can become an addiction, something we go to for compulsive reasons, not simply as fuel for our bodies. Ask yourself: are you in control? We realise that for some men, being round and slightly overweight is part of your persona. There's a safe, unthreatening element to your physical appearance which has served you well and provided a way to connect with people. Lean, muscular, athletic types tend to be more serious and less fun than their playful, slightly rounder counterparts, as a rule. There's nothing wrong with either of these types, and we wouldn't want to radically change the person you feel yourself to be. All we would say is keep an eye on your consumption – on what you're eating and how much and why. You don't want to be that father chasing around an Aldi check-out unable to catch his six year old kid.

*

Yes & No
In general, this chapter is about your 'yes' and your 'no' and finding the balance about what you say each one to and how often. We would encourage you to say 'yes' to a few more things to which you have never had or done before...and 'no' to a few of the things that you always have or do, perhaps in excess.

That's kind of it. Simple, huh?

Remember, we are not the experts on this, and we don't want to offer you any specifics; those are for you to work out for yourself. But we *are* encouraging you to seek balance in this part of your life. Extremes at either end of the spectrum are unlikely to prove truly fun or healthy – physically, mentally, socially – in the long run.

Own who you are.

Take control. Get a grip.

Eat less. Move more.

Enjoy what you have.

Chapter Six

FIRST & LAST

What is success? What does it look like for you?

Imagine for a moment the life of a man who is fixed only upon his career. He starts with some potential. He follows his chosen path – earning more money, climbing up the rungs of his profession, earning still more and more as the years go by, until he becomes very rich. He goes on into his later years, becoming richer and richer still, until eventually he dies.

If that's all that happened in the man's life, if all he achieved was the accumulation of wealth, would we tell stories about him? Would he be remembered?

He's hardly an object of admiration or someone to idolise. He may have been very rich, and his wealth may have brought him a certain amount of power and respect, but without some other component, some other strand to his story, we wouldn't call him great.

Something else has to be there.

That something is what this chapter is about.

When you think about the kind of characters about whom we tell stories, characters we think of as truly great men, there is nearly always some sort of sacrifice woven into their life. A moment when they could have continued along the same path they always walked, but instead they chose another path, one bound in service to others, to something that is greater than themselves. They chose a harder path, often a lower path, and through that found the way to greatness.

We are not suggesting that every man needs to or even should chase greatness. But we are saying that when we think about success, often we limit our thinking to the first example. We think only in one dimension: that personal success means that we work hard, we push ourselves as high as we can go, and so earn the rewards we deserve. But this one-dimensional approach fails to consider the many other dimensions which make a life truly successful. So, if someone was going to write the story of your life, what would they say?

'The last shall be first, and the first last.'

This is one of those sayings that many have heard, but few have taken the time to really examine what it might mean if applied to their own life. We are going to explore how these two opposing concepts, of being first and last, might fit together in the life of the Authentic Man.

*

Inward vs Outward-looking
It is very easy for us to live life only for ourself, putting me/I at the centre of everything.

What do I need? What do I want? What do I hope to achieve? How am I going to reach my goals?

Even after you have formed a long-term relationship with someone, grown a family, created a company, launched a charity – you can still really be living life only for 'me and mine.' The 'I' remains the centre of what you do.

Is that you?

There usually comes a moment in most men's lives when they realise that life is not all about what they can get out of it. At some point they understand that they need to be putting something back in, too.

Work is good. Success is good. Winning is good. But only when this is balanced with serving and giving as well. Achievement and acquisition should be balanced with contribution and connection. Without that, any success you do achieve is likely to feel a hollow and lonely affair. A quote often attributed to Jack Higgins, the international bestselling author, reads, 'What they never tell you is that when you reach the top, there's nothing there.'

So how do you pursue excellence and personal success and still ensure you lead a rich and fulfilling life by giving something back?

Not long after Myles and his wife Becs were married, Becs had just qualified as a barrister and had secured a job with a human rights organisation in Bangalore, India. Myles, meanwhile, intended to try launching a small business out there. In fact, he launched several, initially making sanitary towels out in the rural areas, and after that granola balls, a laundry business and most successfully an office salad catering company.

Some of them went better than others. In any case, his mindset was squarely in the entrepreneurial zone, and he was determined to make some money to support him and his wife. But almost immediately he was struck by an uncomfortable realisation: even at the start of his career with a modest income of around £20K per year, just by moving to the sub-continent he and Becs had leapt from being middle-class average income earners in the UK to being in the top 1% economic demographic in India. The vast majority of people around him had far, far less than him. And yet here he was trying to start a business in order to make some money off them. Seeing that level of poverty on a daily basis changed his attitude profoundly. (So much so he has 'Remember the Poor' tattooed on his chest.)

He was often trying to do things to help them or else help his conscience – there are always dual motives.

His birthday fell about three months after they had moved to Bangalore. Myles decided he was going to throw a party. He called up some caterers and arranged for them to set up an outdoor event, serving biryani to a hundred and twenty people in the car park outside their apartment block. It was only going to cost him around £80 to cover the whole meal.

The day arrived and the caterers got busy setting up tables and chairs around the car park and laying out the placings. At the appointed hour, a handful of Myles' friends arrived, but far fewer than the hundred and twenty people the caterers were expecting. With the meal now ready, the head caterer came to Myles somewhat disgruntled. 'We are ready. Where are all the guests?' he asked.

'Great,' Myles replied. 'Right. Just give me a few minutes.'

He then set off round the local neighbourhood inviting anyone he could find to his birthday party, repeating a phrase he'd learned in Kanada (the local language), 'It's my birthday. Come and have lunch.' Many accepted his invitation, neighbours and shop owners, including some of the most wretched beggars living in the area. Some had no legs; some were blind. But they all made their way to the tables. When they did so, the caterers were horrified. They approached Myles and complained bitterly that they were of high Brahmin caste, whilst the beggars and other local poor were nearly all of the lowest possible caste. The 'untouchables', as they are unflatteringly called. The caterers didn't want to have anything to do with them. But Myles pushed back, saying since he was the one paying for the party, it was up to him who came to it. To that, the caterers offered no rebuttal – seemed they were happy enough to take his money.

Most of the food went. Some people took bags of it home for later. It was a very happy day which Myles still remembers with fondness. To this day, he reckons it the best birthday he's ever had. And he learned a precious lesson that day: that sometimes the best thing you can do with the things you cherish the most – in this case, his birthday and his money – is to give them away. He found doing so to be the most joyous experience. The guests were also happy, and from then on, Myles became known around the area with great affection. That wasn't why he did it, but it was a happy result which he felt for a long time afterwards.

£80 isn't a lot of money to achieve all that, is it?

*

Money
Here's some advice from John Wesley: 'Earn as much as you can. Save as much as you can. Give away as much as you can.'

It sounds simple. And in some ways, it's all you need

to know when it comes to having a healthy attitude to money.

We want to assert that successful men work. But what you then do with the fruits of your labour and how you perceive your work are very different questions.

Often the sense of worth we feel from our work can be confused with the worth we feel from the money that our work produces. For some, your worth as a man equates to the figure in your bank account. Your value as a human being matches your net worth as an individual. Superficial and crass though this idea should seem, you'd be surprised how easily it slips into all of our thinking. For some this is more overt than others.

If someone really believes that their worth is determined by the amount of money they have, you can see why that would cause them to hold onto their money at all costs. What Myles' story shows is that being first doesn't mean you need to remain as rich as you possibly could be by hoarding all that you earn. In any case, being rich or poor is not a binary thing. You can be financially rich, and still be morally bankrupt. And if you're financially poor, you can be richer in other ways. As you well know, often those with less have learned to value more whatever they do have – be it family, or time, the simple joys of good food or nature or friendship or whatever.

It is a truism of the songs and stories of our culture that having money isn't everything. Money can't buy you love. Money doesn't guarantee you happiness. The love of money is the root of all evil. The richest people are often the most broken and desperately unhappy. After all, if you've got everything and it's still not enough, where do you go from there?

Yet even though we all know this to be true, we still allow our souls to be caught between these two grindstones of success and money. We think more money equates to success and that in order to be happy and fulfilled we therefore need to be successful.

But what if you have the power to redefine what it means to be successful?

What if happiness in life is not about what you acquire but what you appreciate?

Think about that. Then think about how you are living your life. What are your objectives and why?

Are you simply trying to acquire more money, more stuff? Do you appreciate the things that you already have, or are you miserable and frustrated because you feel entitled to more things but you don't yet have them?

When you consider these questions, you begin to see why simply having more money is not necessarily the best thing that can happen to you. Happiness has more to do with what you value in life and not what you possess.

*

Earn As Much As You Can...
None of this is supposed to put you off from working hard. Good discipline and a hard work ethic can create a good life, which is clearly a good thing. But it is not enough on its own. You need to bring the right attitude with you as well, as you develop

and grow in your chosen career or profession.

Working hard has served both of us well. It has supported the route to whatever measure of financial success we have enjoyed in life. We have both chosen to make a living based on multiple income streams rather pushing one career to the exclusion of all others. And we have conscientiously created those different streams and work hard to keep them healthy.

But we have found that, even with relatively modest goals when it comes to acquiring wealth, like an insidious worm, money has a way of burrowing into you. It has a magnetic power that can easily take over your life. As the medieval writer Chaucer warned, the desire for more money is at the root of all evil. Greed has driven some of the greatest evils humanity has ever known. We should be honest with ourselves: we are susceptible to dishonesty when it comes to money.

So how do we protect ourselves from corruption?

One of the best ways of making sure that it's you who has control over your money and not the other way round is to give it away. Be open with it. Use it wisely.

*

...Give it away
James has a friend called Mike (not his real name). He's the most generous person James knows, as well as one of the richest. The way Mike hosts is so open, so without limit or qualification, that his relationship with money feels genuinely free.

As his guest, whatever he has, you can have.

Once you have grasped his sincerity in this, it becomes truly inspiring and empowering to witness. When he goes to a restaurant, he immediately wants everyone to have anything and everything that they want. It doesn't matter how many join the party, whether they are his friends or he's never met them before.

It's not unusual to come across generous people, but often they have underlying reasons for their generosity. There are strings attached. Either they are creating a social debt of some kind, expected to be repaid at a later date. Or else they are really organising their own fun – gathering people around them to serve their own ego or create a party atmosphere or whatever. It's not you they are thinking of, but themselves. Or, at the very least, they expect you to be grateful to them afterwards, to note them for their generosity. The end goal is for you to notice them, be impressed by them and to honour them.

With Mike, there are no strings attached. When James asked him how he made sense of this approach, his reply was as revealing as it was inspiring. The answer lies, he explained, in the value that he puts on friendship and connection within the group. It didn't matter whether that connection was with close friends or people who had just met. For him, those things were so valuable that they literally had no price. However much money he spent facilitating that, both for himself and for other people, what it cost him was irrelevant when considered against what we all stood to gain from the mutual connections in the room.

That is such a liberating and rare attitude. We may not all have the money that Mike has to spend on bringing people together, but we can at least share in his attitude.

As much as he aspires to be like Mike, James is embarrassed to say that there is still a long way to go in this regard. On one occasion, recently, in which James was called upon to be generous, he showed how, by being too attached to the money he was spending – even in an act of generosity – you can ruin the experience of giving something away.

On this particular occasion, he was driving back in a full car with his two sons and some of their friends. They stopped off at a McDonalds drive-thru, and James called back to the excited boys in the car for their orders. He was expecting each kid to ask for a Big Mac meal or something equivalent, and he was happy to pay for it all. But when each boy started throwing forward various add-ons – extra milk shakes, McFlurries, a box of donuts here, six extra nuggets there, and so on – his indignation started to rise. Whatever the extra amount came to – probably no more than fifteen quid – it was enough to put him into a stinking mood for the rest of the drive home, which was all too evident to his passengers. It wasn't the money that bothered him so much as the liberty that these kids had taken with his 'generosity', and he couldn't shift the cloud of resentment for the rest of the day. He just wasn't expecting them to take his offer of 'What do you all want?' that literally. What should have been a fun day out ended on a very sour note.

This moment highlights the challenge; if you are going to be generous, you have to go all in. No strings attached; no expectations for something in return; a sheer act of giving as pure as you can make it. And if you offer kindness, give it. All in.

Myles married into a family who did a lot better in this area. Often on a Sunday, the impromptu list of people invited back for a Sunday roast grew pretty big. Way bigger than the amount of food Becs' Mum had prepared. As more and more people arrived, and the time came for the food to be served, Becs' Dad would often arrive with another random person. Myles is quite into his food, counting his macros, calculating his protein intake. He would start to panic that there wasn't enough. But jostling with the mini FOMO explosion in his head, there is a silent family rule which says, 'Family hold back.' Although it's rarely explicitly stated, you soon figure out that it's there. Myles would watch his brother-in-law and wife take a tiny little portion after all the guests had taken their food; Becs' mum and dad would take theirs last, making sure all their guests had enough. Myles, meanwhile, had already heaped his plate high. But in spite of his full belly, he was left with the hollow feeling that maybe he had missed something important.

It took Myles a while to get the point. Do you want to be the host that no one wants to have lunch with or the one who sends friends away with a full belly?

*

Men Hold Back
Through being generous, you are putting yourself last.

The idea of 'family hold back' could point the way towards how men could lead in this area.

How about the Authentic Man hold back? What would that look like – in your marriage, in your family, in your community? In your school, in your company, in your industry? In the wider world?

The reality for most of us is that we could travel a long way in that direction before we reach where we probably ought to be. Let's blow the lid on it, man to man. Our spending on ourselves is often way higher than anything we complain about in our female partners, in our sisters or our mothers.

Think about men's sports events, for example. Most men keep the level of spending on this kind of thing pretty well hidden. But these days if you go to watch a top flight game, have a few drinks with your mates and a bite to eat afterwards, you're unlikely to see much change out of £200. Probably you could see the same game for free on TV. Essentially that's £200 swallowed up into the ether. So when our partner spends £200 on a new item of clothing, do we have any right to complain? At least she looks good with it, and she'll probably enjoy it and use it forty or fifty times. More than can be said for the seven pints of lager you drank last night.

There's a challenge there about how we use our money.

Men hold back.

*

Being Seen To Be First
In the chapter on Right & Wrong, we have already pointed out how ugly it feels when a man needs to be seen to be right. Well, the same is true when he

wants to be seen to be first.

The guy who wants to parade all the outward trappings of his wealth and worldly success as a mark of his supposed superiority. The sports cars, expensive watches, designer labels, you name it. What you might call flash spending. Or showing off.

It's all relative, of course. You don't need to own a private jet to be showing off. Among your own peer group, you can probably think of the equivalent. Maybe it's where you go on holiday. Maybe it's the car you drive. There is likely a guy on your street who does this all the time.

Just make sure it's not you.

There's no need to show off your alleged prowess to everyone around you. There's no need to assert your place in the pecking order. Instead take a step back rather than a step forward.

We should be comfortable letting someone else show themselves off without seething with resentment or without our competitive nerve twitching to get in the game. We should be comfortable with letting someone else hold forth about their success at work without having to overlay our own achievements in response.

*

What Does Putting Yourself Last Look Like?
We've all got different motives that we cling to.

Some of us need to feel safe and secure. Others want to be noticed. Some crave power. Some of us just want someone's approval. And still others are desperate to win.

So what does putting yourself last look like?

Maybe taking a risk on behalf of someone else or speaking out when it's safer to stay silent. Maybe it's being ignored or not pulling focus when it's someone else's moment to shine. Maybe it's letting someone else take charge, giving up power and control when you'd rather keep hold of it yourself. Maybe it's doing something you know is the right thing to do, even if it forfeits another's approval. Maybe it's losing for once and doing it with good grace.

It'll be different for each of us. And harder depending on what it is.

Recently James was away on a long weekend with some of his mates. One morning they were preparing a slap-up breakfast. James was on coffees. Another friend, Tom, was making pancakes. When it came to making up James' plate, Tom kept asking him his preferences. Did he want warm syrup? Yes, he did. Did he want warm clotted cream poured over the pancakes? Yes, he did. Did he want extra berries and banana slices? Yes, of course he did. By the time he was done, there was a mountainous mouth-watering dish waiting for James to tuck into. James lay his plate down on the table and went back to the kitchen to get the coffees. Returning to his place, he found another friend already pulling out the chair and sliding his legs under the table. Despite his urge to speak up, James kept his mouth shut and went back out to the kitchen to prepare himself another plate of food. Cold syrup, cold cream, no berries left, no bananas. Having surrendered his specially prepared breakfast to this other bloke, it took all the willpower he had in him not to say, 'By the way, that's my breakfast you're eating, mate.

Enjoy!'

It would have been the easiest thing in the world to tell him, as mouthfuls of pancake and syrup and clotted cream disappeared down his neighbour's gullet. But also the ugliest. Happily he resisted the temptation this time. But it was undeniably hard.

Perhaps this is a trivial example. But it shows how, even in the smallest moments in life, there is still ample opportunity to put others first and ourselves last. And that guy clearly enjoyed his breakfast.

*

The Other Extreme - Last
Having laid out the case against putting yourself first all the time, we also need to point out that you can go too far the other way as well.

There was a man whom James used to work with who would put himself last in all things at all times. It became his virtue signal, if you like; his crumb of comfort in the face of always having the worst of it. Or giving himself the worst of it. The problem was there was a strong seam of self-righteousness running through everything he did. He was proud that he gave himself the worst of everything; that bad things always seemed to happen to him; that he was last and would always be the last. (There was more than a hint of self-sabotage about him, too, so that his doom-saying became a self-fulfilling prophecy.) At any company event, he would purposefully wait until everyone else had eaten before he ate. He would turn up early to meetings and events long before he needed to. He did all the dirty jobs on his own without waiting for help. But boy, did he make sure everyone knew it. And that was the give-away.

One of Charles Dickens's most famous novels is *David Copperfield*. The antagonist of the story is a young clerk called Uriah Heep who is continually describing himself as 'ever so 'umble.' In fact, the man is not humble at all but full of wounded pride. It's his defining characteristic. He feels like the world has wronged him and that this gives him licence to wrong the world right back. James' work colleague was a bit like that. Many people are.

Much of what has become known as virtue signalling today is far more about pride and self-aggrandisement than actually helping others. That's what makes it so distasteful. People who make a show of representing others who are struggling to burnish their own credentials as a 'good person' but, in fact, do very little to actually alleviate the situation.

The person who insists on always being seen to be last actually has more in common with the man roaring up and down the street in his Ferrari than you might think. They are two sides of the same coin. The coin represents pride: thinking too much of yourself. High-achievers can be proud, always pushing to be first. Low-achievers can also be proud, always making a show of being last or else the victim.

Both of these are wrong.

We would encourage men to get in the habit of thinking of themselves less (a point we make in the chapter on Right & Wrong). We would argue that humility (the opposite of pride) means being both first and last all of the time. Having sufficient self-respect that you don't need to stick out of the crowd – either at one end or the other – in order to feel good about yourself.

Once more it's about balance. Living with an element of sacrifice, of living for others over yourself, but not making sacrifice your obsession.

James' mother was a vegetarian long before it became a trendy food fad, as was her own mother before her. She was very disciplined about maintaining that diet. But James witnessed her time and again laying aside that commitment when she was a guest in another person's house. Not wanting to make any kind of fuss or draw attention to herself, she would instead eat as much of whatever her hosts had kindly provided her as she could and just leave aside the parts she really couldn't face. That, also, is an example of putting herself last. Laying aside a principle that was important to her to avoid her host's discomfort or inconvenience.

*

Balance And Success
We hope it goes without saying that being successful is a reasonable goal. And no example of success comes without some kind of sacrifice. It demands effort and time and determination – blood, sweat and often tears. The question is, in order to attain success, have you sacrificed the right things or the wrong things?

For example, has a man's success come at the cost of his relationship with his children? Has he trampled on his friends to reach the top?

Maybe success is not only about your career but about what kind of a father you are, what kind of a partner, and what kind of a friend.

The irony that most of us discover is that even as our careers progress, and we start to earn a bit more money, as our income goes up, so too do our costs. In a superficial sense, all we're doing is moving up the supermarket chain – from Lidl and Morrisons at one end, towards the lofty heights of Waitrose and M&S at the other. But a pint of milk is still just a pint of milk. We use it in our coffee or on our cornflakes. And yet we end up buying milk from different supermarkets until we've risen right out of the supermarket altogether, and get it delivered to our door, straight from the cow's udder. Then we know we've made it!

You can begin to see the absurdity of it.

The key questions to ask are, how much do you really need to earn? How much do you really need to spend? How much can you save? And can you give more away?

You play an important role. Your community needs your input. They need you to put something back. So maybe instead of committing to sitting on a company advisory committee for the kudos it gives you, what if you volunteered at your local school to become a governor instead? What if you helped out with the local food bank or scout troop?

These are just simple suggestions, but they give you some idea where you might make a start.
Your personal success is only part of the picture. It's

what you do with it that really counts.

*

Sacrifice
Great leadership often looks like sacrifice. Think of the Spartan kings who always stood in the first line of battle. Think of the Samurai who longs for a heroic death in service of others. Think of the Knights of the Round Table, men of honour, fighting and dying for a noble cause. Think of the junior officers leading the charge in the First and Second World Wars.

These are the men who can teach us something about how to live (and in some cases die) well. Too often these days our leaders look to their own fame and reputation and their own comfort, paying lip service to the poor and vulnerable about whom they don't really care other than as a political launch-pad to advance their own careers.

Don't be like that.

We can be different.

We can be both first and last.

Our lives can become a story worth telling.

Chapter Seven

SONS & FATHERS

One title which we all share as men is *son*. Whether we like the role or not, whatever it has come to mean for us, every single one of us is a son. We might not all be fathers. We might not all be husbands. We might not all be brothers. But we are all sons.

Sonship is a birthright, a mantle which rests on any male infant from the moment he is conceived. It is something you inherit and also something you grow into.

In this chapter, we want to explore what it means to be a son.

But also we want to explore what it means to be a *father*. And how these two identities weave together.

To make sense of this, we have found a concept known as the *Hero's Journey* useful. This describes the progression from apprentice to hero to guide. Or put another way, from Padawan to Jedi to Jedi Master.

Here's what we mean.

*

The Hero's Journey
This was a concept originally articulated by the mythologist Joseph Campbell in his 1949 book *The Hero With A Thousand Faces*. It has to do with the archetypes of myth and storytelling, common

threads which, he asserts, seem to run through all human stories from whichever culture, whichever era they arose. It's something Campbell calls the 'monomyth.'

He saw a common shape and structure to stories, which, according to his model, took the form of a sequential journey. It provided a framework of understanding story, which the storytellers of the modern age have returned to again and again. Hollywood, especially, has been influenced by his thinking. So it's unsurprising that most of the movies we grew up with are saturated with this model. You may have never heard of the Hero's Journey, but we bet you've watched it a thousand times.

Perhaps the most famous example in movie-making of the Hero's Journey is the original *Star Wars* movie, released in 1977. The writer/director George Lucas followed Joseph Campbell's model very closely in formulating the story of his hero, Luke Skywalker. One of the reasons *Star Wars* was such a knockout success, and went on to birth its own subculture, is that it touched something very deep in the human psyche. It was a faithful retelling of the archetypal monomyth.

And the reason stories like *Star Wars* strike such a chord in us is that the archetypes of story are really the archetypes of life. Let's unpack that journey.

The hero finds himself born into this world.

Something happens. A trigger. He receives a call to adventure – often towards a beauty to win, a mission to accomplish, a battle to fight or a reward to attain. Many times the hero resists that call at first. Often he meets with a mentor at this point who gives him the wisdom and encouragement that he needs. And if the call is insistent enough, the hero gathers his courage and embarks on the adventure. Entering a new and unknown world, he learns to develop and harness his skills, moving towards his goal. He meets with allies and enemies, forces that try to block his progress. He faces ordeals – challenges he must overcome – which will test his resolve and his resourcefulness to their limits. At last he faces the ultimate test from the forces ranged against him, which are trying to thwart the attainment of his goal. If he passes the test, he returns home with his reward, wiser and stronger, and a different man to the young hero who first set out. His adventure, what he has learned and become, now benefits his community and his world.

That, in a nutshell, is the Hero's Journey.

The reason we have unpacked this in a bit of detail here is because it reflects our experience of life. Understanding the Hero's Journey helps us better to make sense of our life and our shifting roles within it. And in particular, we think it is applicable when we are looking at what it means to be both a son and a father.

In these relational roles, we find ourselves at different points in our lives playing the story roles of apprentice, hero and guide.

There is a difference though. The development in stories tends to be linear, moving on from one role to the next. The more we looked at applying this thinking to real life, the more we realised men are actually playing all of these roles, to a greater or lesser extent, throughout their life, all of the time.

So, although you might not yet have fathered your own child, that doesn't mean you cannot 'father' other boys or men in your life (leading them into knowledge and wisdom, encouraging them in their adventures). By contrast, whilst you may be expert in certain fields, wise and experienced in others, you still have scope to be a total novice – a Padawan – in new things and many other areas of your life. There is something about our youth – about the playfulness and fun of being a boy – that should be carried on into adulthood, which we don't want to lose.

So remember, before all else and until your dying day, you will be a son.

*

Becoming The Hero
As the theory goes, you cannot become a hero or a guide unless you've been through the Hero's Journey yourself. As kids, we all find ourselves in the Padawan stage. We are naturally apprentices in life. We are looking around, soaking up knowledge and experience, acquiring skills, but without the focus and sense of goal and purpose which will launch us into our own Hero's Journey.

Usually, around the teenage years, something shifts.

Both young men and women develop a more acute sense that they actually want to do something with their lives. That they are going to change the world somehow. And for young men, in particular, often this feels like they want to become the hero of their own story. That shift within our will and our identity can be a powerful driver towards realising our dreams.

Responsibility

When Myles was a teenager he had one such dream for his life. He thought if he could find some beauty whom he could love, if he could win her heart, be worthy of her, if he could marry and take care of her, then he would be a hero. If he could succeed in that, then surely he could succeed in anything and would be well on the way to becoming a guide to others.

It's a classic motive: the impulse of romance, to win the Beauty's heart. It forms the spine of many a romcom and epic romance plot.

When Myles first saw Becs he knew he would marry her. Or he wanted to anyway. From their second date he started saving for an engagement ring. His housemates told him he was a stalker. Maybe he was a little bit. But it's a thin line between stalker and pursuer and the beginning of an epic love story.

Although the challenge to get her to notice him seemed insurmountable. They came from vastly different friendship groups. Different classes. It felt like a huge gap between him and her. Not to mention she was part of an old tightknit church community, where the children of children marry their friends children, or god children, etc. He was also a bit chippy about these 'Hoorah Henrys.' (Now has a brother in law called Henry, who he loves!)

You get it. But he saw her. And that was it for him. He was so convinced that who you marry has the biggest impact on your life and happiness, so why wouldn't he pursue the best possible girl he could find? The hottest, the coolest, the most interesting. And Becs was it. Trouble is, she was also protected by a venomous gaggle of girls, as sassy and beautiful as they were notorious at destroying a man's reputation. They even had a nickname for them-selves which others soon referred to as 'Kavos' – it was basically a verb, clever branding; a gang, a warning.

Now, it has to be made known that Becs had spotted Myles a long way back, even before he had laid eyes on this old testament style Jewish looking beauty, he later learned was called Rebecca. And she liked what she saw. In fact, she loved it. She told a Kavos friend 'he's perfect' – and then promptly locked away all traces of these feelings far away from Myles. So even though the gap between them looked impossible and all the bookies wrote him off, this just made the challenge even greater. Myles would battle through an armada of snobby looks and rejection until he had made her his wife. And even now she still plays hard to get. She could have made it a whole lot easier. But this would have not allowed Myles to go on the Hero's Journey. To go from Padawan to Jedi Master.

Sweep through the burning eyes of Kavos and emerge as the hero who won her heart.

They went on several dates. The engagement ring was as good as bought. And then one day as they were walking in the park, the birds tweeting, the sun shining, he mentioned he was going to get his haircut the next day (good chat) and asked what her feelings were about this, and if she wanted to have any input on the style. To which she replied 'No. And I don't want to see you again,' and immediately walked off to a bar to do what Kavos girls do when a guy gets burned by them. The posh version of a high five for girls, whatever that looks like.

It was over. Gone. Finished. Aiming for a central London metro chick was clearly too high an aspiration for guys like him. Maybe he should head back to the suburbs and aim for a mid-level wife from the tier 2 commuter town he grew up in: Slough ('just outside Windsor,' which makes it sound more classy).

He cried on the phone to a friend. Devastated. Broken and defeated. Keith asked him, 'Is that it mate? You gonna' give up that easily?' At this moment he was the guide to Myles. Keith was a bit older and was happily married to an amazing woman. Already weathered in the Hero's Journey, having been on it himself many years before. Keith gave him the pre battle speech, hyped him up a bit and several weeks later Myles swaggered into the middle of a Kavos circle, chest puffed out, head high – but with zero actual confidence inside. With a look, one of the girls insinuated, 'What are you doing here, Loser? Haven't you learned your lesson?' Ignoring the screaming desire to run away, Myles thrust out his hand and said to Becs, 'Let's get out of here.' In those few seconds the air felt like it was sucked out of the room, while Kavos paused to see Becs' reaction before they pounced.

'Okay' she said. Myles took her hand, and they rode off into the night on his 50cc scooter.

The rest is kind of history. It had its ups and downs, as it always does.

In a recent coaching/therapy session. Myles was asked what some of his greatest achievements were, and he had to write them down on a white board. Number one: marrying Becs. Hands down. Hero's Journey. And now he has been through it. He feels like he could be the Keith to someone else one day.

At least to his own sons when they fall in love with a rare beauty.

What James loves about this story was Myles' willingness to go all in at the pivotal moment. Myles focused on Becs, even though he was still relatively young. He was committed to go after his goal and overcome the barriers that stood before him. Too often, as men, we may want something or someone, but we are not brave enough to step into it. Too afraid to answer the call to adventure.

Of course, if it were a movie, the closing shot would be Becs walking down the aisle to an ecstatic Myles, with the suggestion that they would now live happily ever after. And then the credits would roll.

But the reality is that Myles entered a story that would go on for as long as they both live – to discover what it means to become a man and husband worthy of the amazing woman he had won over.

'Winning the Beloved' is an archetypal goal that is as old as storytelling itself. And every story needs a goal – however big or small. Without one, there literally is no story. You can't have a narrative without a dramatic aim. We think that, to be the Authentic Man, you should be adding a bit of narrative to your story every day. The hero of any story must be active, applying themselves towards achieving a goal. If they aren't, the story fails. And if we as men aren't doing that, life will stall as well. Vague or unclear goals weaken a story. The clearer and more defined the goal, the greater the hero's drive towards it.

The reason we start with this idea in this chapter is

that we think this could be the answer to one of the questions of life for us as men: What's our point? What are we here for?

*

Good Heroes Become Guides
As we said, what unites us is that we are all sons. But it's also likely that many of us will be actual biological fathers, too. There is a call, then, for us not only to be heroes, but also to be guides. Maybe you already have children, in which case you're already expected to be a hero and guide to them. If you don't yet, maybe one day you will. Or in the meantime, perhaps you have other dependents – nephews, nieces, godchildren, younger kids in your community. It's a rare man that doesn't have someone looking to him for an example. We are all leaders in the sense that we all influence other people. The question then arises: are we a good influence or a bad one?

The heroes of our culture become examples to the rest of us, showing us in different ways how we should live our lives. In an ideal world, their heroism should be sort of contagious. Their courage calling forth the courage in our own hearts to urge and inspire us towards our own goals. Towards fighting our own demons, slaying our own dragons.

And as fathers, we want to be heroes to our children. But we don't only want to be heroes to them. Good fathers also go on to be guides to their younger Padawans, so they too may one day grow into becoming heroes.

Myles was once on holiday with his family in Corfu.

One day they visited a part of the island where people would swim out to a cliff face, climb up the rocks and then jump off into the water. Most people jumped from the lower level. But there was another jump about five meters higher up from which anyone attempting the jump had to launch themselves outwards far enough to clear a projection of rock below if they were to make it into the water.

As their boat approached the cliff, Myles and his family watched two lads of around twenty climb up to the top level. But after looking rather gingerly over the edge, they backed out and scrambled back down to the lower level.

'D'you think you can do that top one, Dad?' Myles' son asked him. There was a note of longing in his young voice. And of course, once a child asks a question like that of his father, what could Myles do but put himself to the test?

He swam over and climbed up to the top. Looking down, it certainly felt pretty high. It would take a decent run up and jump to clear the rocks below. But with everyone looking on, including his family and the two lads who had bottled it, he wasn't going to back down now.

So he took a few deep breaths…and jumped.

He missed the cliff edge below by a whisker and smashed hard into the sea, stinging his feet and smacking his ear drum painfully. But when he got back into the boat, his son was leaping around in delight. 'You're a hero, Dad! None of those boys would do it – but *you* did it, Dad!' He was truly impressed and proud of his father. For Myles, it was an undeniably good feeling.

A sweet and memorable moment, but Myles was distinctly aware that the point of being a father is not to bask in the hero worship of your children, nice though that may be. It is to become a guide to them so that one day they may go on to jump off still higher cliffs. That is the beautiful transition, when you pass from hero to guide so that you can help your sons and daughters make the transition from Padawans into Jedis. Apprentices into heroes.

If all you want to do is take the accolades for yourself, thinking 'Yes – aren't I amazing?' then we think you're missing the point. Rather, you should be the father who says, 'One day you can do that – *and more*!'

You are a guide to your Padawans so that they can surpass you, not so they can blow smoke up your arse.

*

Both/And
You may wonder when the moment comes that you transition from being the hero to becoming the guide. And how do you judge when that is?

We think there is a natural place for this. But at the same time, we don't want to be too directive about it. As we said before, when it comes to living out the relationship between father and son, it feels more like a shifting emphasis between the different roles of apprentice, hero and guide.

As with all the other themes in this book, it is both/

and.

Think about when a child is first born. As the father,

immediately you have to do something 'heroic' for them. Like pick them up; change their nappy; support their mum; keep them safe; keep them warm. These are all small things (and no doubt the mother is doing this and far more too). But in all these things, you are acting the role of the hero.

And yet, at the same time, babies immediately start to teach us a few things, too.

They teach us how selfish we are, how stupid we are, how ill-prepared we are, and how insensitive we are. We may want to be our newborn child's hero and guide, but the reality is that they are also teaching us. In small and subtle ways, they are already guiding us. Do you see what we're saying?

And when your child does something impressive for the first time – even if it's swallowing their first mouthful of solid food – your heart swells with that first sense of pride at their accomplishment. As we watch them grow, that natural pride at their achievements, from the smallest step to the greatest leap, never seems to grow old. Often we boast about our children simply because we admire them so much. We are so proud of who they are and how far they've come.

It's both/and.

Check yourself. If all that you've done is build your own hero narrative, then it's time to shine the spotlight on someone else for a change. If not your own children, then who could be your Padawan?

*

Bad Heroes Become The Fool
One of the recurring archetypal themes of story-telling is that the Hero who won't learn becomes the Fool.

Every hero that sets out on an adventure will bring his skills and strengths with him, but he will also bring his weaknesses and his flaws. Often one of the marks of a good character arc in a story is that the hero comes to recognise his own flaws and then seeks to resolve them. Indeed, he must fix them in order to overcome his enemy and achieve his reward. The coward finds his courage. The angry man finds his peace. The cheat becomes honest. The liar tells the truth. The selfish man becomes sacrificial.

But the hero who will not learn from his mistakes and so fix his own flaws is bound to repeat them. And so he becomes the Fool, living life in an endlessly repeating cycle.

Staying teachable is the best way to avoid this happening to you.

As we said again and again in the chapter on Right & Wrong, being humble is crucial because it enables you to ask yourself the question: What am I missing? Where am I the Fool? Asking these questions enables you to be open to gaining wisdom and understanding. They allow you to learn and grow.

Of course, no one wants to be the Fool in their own story. But many men prove to be just that.

James knows a guy who recently sent him a blunt text stating, 'I'm homeless again as of tonight. You don't know anywhere I could stay for a couple of nights, do you? Cheers mate.'

Sadly the backstory to this guy is that he has failed everyone in his life: his wife, his children, and his friends. This is the third time James has received this kind of message. He hears little from this guy in between other than how great he is and how well he's doing. He never asks what's going on in James' life.

On the surface, the man has had some markers of success. A quick glance might suggest he was a man who's got it all together. He boasts about high earnings; he eats at expensive restaurants; he drives expensive cars. But the reality is he has crashed and burned again and again. He only seems to reach out to his friends to ask them to get him out of a hole. When his wife was suffering from cancer, he left her for another woman. He abandoned his teenage children and even stole money from one of them. He has failed those who relied on him. And yet, he has no issues about casually casting about for help from the most random of connections when he needs it.

Over the last few years, he went from being his kids' hero to becoming 'an utter loser' as one of his children described him. The reason? 'He won't learn,' said his son. 'He never learns...he's the worst thing in our lives.'

It's tragic to see this. No one wants a guy to fail so badly in his family life. But all of us need to recognise that we all have flaws, some worse than others. And the worst flaw of all is probably hubris: the idea that nothing could go wrong for you, or that you're fine just the way you are. We all need to face our flaws and set about fixing them. That way, we can continue to build our narrative, and the narrative of those who come after us, in a positive direction.

Stay teachable.

Be the Hero. Not the Fool.

*

What Is Sonship?
We want to return now to the idea of sonship. When we say sonship is a birthright, something we are born into – what exactly is that 'something?'

As children, many of us are naturally adventurous and bold and courageous. We are self-absorbed, but in a beautiful way. Then, as life goes on, we become slowly more and more inhibited. Like a man carrying a rucksack up a hill as more and more things are loaded onto his back, slowing him down, limiting his options and his energy to pursue them.

Children are nothing but potential.

Think back to the young boy and then young man you once were. Reject any victim thinking and imagine the best of you. What was your potential? What were you born into that excited you? Did you sustain that excitement along the way, or did you lay it aside at some point? Too often life comes along and crushes the enthusiasms right out of us.

Sometimes the journey from sonship into fatherhood can lead to us laying aside what we should have retained, but also retaining what we should have laid aside. This can have a massive impact on the kind of man and father we are becoming.

An example of this is connected to the different roles of mother and father in our lives. Both play a huge part in how we will turn out as men and how our own role as a father will unfold.

Obviously this book is geared towards masculinity, so there is a lot more discussion within it about fatherhood. However, the role of mother is also crucial, formative and hugely important. The capacity of a mother to positively influence her child matches that of a father. However, here too there is potential for great harm. Plenty of research demonstrates how over-nurturing by our mothers – also known as a strong mother complex – can stunt our maturation into adult men. So, if a man is to develop into an independent person from his parents, it is important to create a clear break with his dependence on them at some point.

Often this moment may have been marked by some sort of rite of passage – from boyhood into manhood – the substance of which might differ across diverse cultures. Sometimes other cultures achieve this in more overt rituals or ceremonies than our own. But the goal is the same: to separate from the mother's domain (symbolised by the home); and to be welcomed into the domain of men (symbolised by the wild).

It is an important transition and one that, as fathers, we must take responsibility for and initiate.

Research shows that the instinctive nature of motherhood just isn't there in fatherhood. We have to learn how to be good fathers; we have to have it modelled for us. We have to learn how to be a nurturer. Our natural biological instinct is to sow our seed and then wander off, leaving the mother with her natural biological instinct which is to incubate and raise our offspring.

We are not trying to cast simplistic roles here. There is much nuance to what we are saying. Taken out of this context, it may sound that we are manufacturing rather binary roles. However, whilst we believe that we can and must change, and do the things we are not instinctively driven to do, our broader point is that these underlying instincts tell us something about the journey of the Authentic Man. And so we raise them with that in mind.

This transition into adulthood is an opportunity for fathers to play a significant role in the development of their children. These days many things could represent a rite of initiation into adulthood. In the past, this may have been the first time a boy hunted and killed something; or the first time he went into battle; or the first time he survived a storm in a boat. Interestingly, anthropologists find that it is often the case that women are banned from witnessing these moments. Perhaps an implicit recognition that this is not the moment for nurturing; rather it's a time to send the young boy/man out into the wild.

Overt rites of passage are a rarity now in our western culture, but that does not diminish their importance. Often we replace them with unofficial 'rites of passage,' which aren't very helpful. Your first cigarette. Your first beer. The first time you get laid. Your first fist-fight. Within gang culture, such initiations can get far, far worse. The problem here isn't so much the activities themselves but that they are usually in the context of big kids initiating smaller kids into an adolescent view of adulthood. In other words, they're ineffective as a true rite of passage. And ineffective rites of passage create a smoke-screen. They create the illusion that a boy has in fact grown up, when really they've done nothing of the sort. Instead, they become a sort of stunted adult, stuck in what psychologists called Peter Pan Syndrome (the *Puer Aeternus*). The boys who never grew up. You probably know some men like that. Hopefully you're not one of them.

But ask yourself the question – am I too shielded by one or both of my parents? Am I looking for a life partner who will mother me?

In other words: am I sure that I grew up? Or am I stuck in Neverland with the other Lost Boys?

*

Sons To Fathers - Taking Responsibility
Our underlying view is that rites of passage are fundamentally about giving and taking responsibility.

Such responsibility might be a heavy burden or it may be a light one. Often boys and young men reach a point in their lives when they naturally want to take some responsibility on their own shoulders. But if they are never given this responsibility, or it is soon taken back off them, this will stunt them, inhibiting their development into fully functioning adult men.

Taking responsibility is a crucial step for the Authentic Man.

Is my bed made? Are my clothes clean? Is my bank account healthy? Do I have a job? Do I have a career? Do I have a decent place to live? Do I have a partner and a family? Does my roof need fixing?

Does my marriage need fixing? Does my community need fixing? Does my world need fixing? Do I need fixing?

It starts with me.

Without responsibility, you remain a boy forever. A Peter Pan, floating around Neverland with the other Lost Boys, chasing after Tinkerbell the fairy, who represents the fantasy image of women, the kind of women whose beauty is as fleeting as fairy dust. And all the while you have the more obvious choice of a Wendy waiting for you. A dependable, responsible woman – a wife and a mother with her feet on the ground. The one who has a good and kind heart who will grow up with you and age with you properly. Of course, the joke is that it's not as if Tinkerbell is a real choice. She doesn't even exist!

When we have tried to 'self-initiate' into manhood – with drink, drugs, porn or other ways of generally making a nuisance of ourselves – those things stay with us and become a marker of our Peter Pan Syndrome. When you first get your driving licence and get your first car, most young men drive around too fast, blaring loud music out of the windows. Maybe that's normal for youths aged 17 or 18. But if you're still doing that at 30 or even older, we have a problem. When we first did them for the first time, these kinds of things signalled that we were now grown up. But if you are still doing them 20 years later, such things in fact become a marker of our *failure* to grow up.

Responsibility is the marker of a son becoming a father, of a boy becoming a man. But that doesn't mean that there aren't certain aspects of our boyhood that we cannot bring with us into

manhood, as we've said. A sense of playfulness and fun. We don't want to lose that.

But often we kill that sense of child-like fun with over-seriousness. There is an innocence we can inherit from our own childhood that is precious. Don't let go of that. We should never lose the adolescent sense that the world is my oyster and we can step into it. A sense of possibility joined with a sense of responsibility is a potent combination for living a successful and fulfilling life.

*

Responsibility & Father Wounds

Fathers matter.

There are enough statistics out there that we can take the following opinion to be as good as fact: *healthy fathers create healthy families and healthy communities*. Therefore, we need healthy fathers. But these are not going to come about if we don't know how to transition from sonship into fatherhood well.

As we said, underlying the transition is this idea of taking responsibility. Perhaps the single greatest arena of life in which men have failed to take responsibility is the world of sex.

Sleep around a bit, and you'll soon discover that it's

actually easy to become a father. It's simple biology. But if you're unready or unwilling to take responsibility for children, then this behaviour leads to terrible outcomes. One in four pregnancies are aborted today in the UK. In 2021, there were on average over 600 hundred abortions every day.

Wherever you stand on the issue of abortion, that is a lot of blood on the hands of men unwilling to take responsibility for the children they have created. And even if the child is born, fatherlessness is often cited as the single biggest cause of brokenness in our society.

Here's the reality: if you feel free to have sex with whoever will have you, you need to be prepared for the consequences. We would suggest that if you're not ready to have a child with every person you are sleeping with, then you shouldn't be having sex at all.

Recently, we took two hundred men away to the wilds of Dartmoor on an XCC. The theme of the weekend was 'fatherhood'. It was a sober reminder of how real and widespread what is sometimes called the 'father wound' is in men. We heard stories covering just about every area of life – some which anyone could see would have left a wound on the son in question; others were more personal to that person's own sensibilities. They ranged from sexual or physical abuse, to abandonment, to a harsh word at just the wrong moment. All of these strike at the heart of the son. And instead of being the wise mentor providing encouragement and support for the hero then to venture out on his quest, the father becomes the dark shadow cast over the hero's life.

(You only have to think of the contrast between Obi-Wan Kenobi and Darth Vader to recognise the difference.)

Even the best of us has a tendency to abdicate our responsibilities as a father too readily. Because, as we've said, it doesn't come naturally in the same way that maternal instincts come. We lose interest,

we get sucked into the vortex of our own vices, and the noble responsibility of being a father is simply left alone.

Left undone.

*

Father To Many
The role of father has tremendous significance whether it is done well or done poorly. That is why we encourage men to do it well, but also we want to suggest that there's no reason you should limit being a father to your own offspring. Rather, look around you. Ask yourself. Who else could I father? Who's looking for a guide? Who could I help empower? What good could I call out of them? What support can I give them?

Be intentional.

Look around. Notice. Engage.

Recently James was on holiday in the Alps. He witnessed a boy falling off a ski drag-lift. The boy slid down the slope, completely out of control, skis and poles flying everywhere. Within seconds, a man immediately behind him on the lift – not his own father – dropped off the lift and skied down to help the boy. He straightened him out, got him back on his skis, then escorted him down to the bottom of the lift and accompanied him back up to the top on the same T-bar, to reunite with his parents. In that moment, the man had been a father to that boy. All it took was an alertness to the world around him and a willingness to help. His response appeared instinctive. But probably it's taken years of choosing to help over choosing to ignore for that choice to become an instinct.

It's ironic that this instinct doesn't come naturally to men. It has to be developed and honed. Our hope for you is that reading this book provides some kind of help in this. But you can also help yourself. Make a practice of thinking well of other people. Make a practice of encouraging others. Make a practice of taking a step forward instead of a step back.

At the end of it all, you may not get a medal. But you will be closer to becoming the Authentic Man.

Let's face it. Fathering in any form is a privilege and you can have great impact. Consider it like this, if you have just one child, then your influence over the earth has just doubled. If you have two children, it has multiplied again. And so on.

So if you're looking for purpose in life and you have kids, then look no further than them. You have more than enough purpose in those younger lives to change the world forever.

Imagine if every man looked after his children, paid attention to them and raised them well. How much we would impact the world for the better?

Often the problem is that we abdicate our responsibility to those close around us in favour of trying to change the world further away on our own. We may have set up umpteen charities for good causes, or built up businesses that will take over the world, but at home our kids are running riot, or feeling lost, unsupported and abandoned.

This is the challenge for men.

How do we remain heroes and guides all the way through our stories?

How do we father well?

It's important to remind ourselves, if we are a father and not doing such a great job, there is still time to change. While there is still breath in our body, there is time to change.

Start now. Take control. Take the initiative. Add narrative to the story of your life. Be intentional.

Many societies cry out for a modern template for a rite of passage. Killing an animal is no longer appropriate or very necessary. Having your first shag is totally against what we've been saying throughout the book. Getting drunk for the first time – or even having your first beer – is really just a small moment. Essentially it's insignificant; you don't need your dad to have your first beer.

No. We want to suggest a more intentional approach that is both more significant and yet more mundane.

We think maturity and responsibility go hand in hand, and that another way to talk about responsibility is to speak of *dominion*.

*

Dominion
If we were to ask you what you are responsible for, you might say, my family, my car, my van, my desk, my garden shed, my dog, etc. That is what you have dominion over. We talk about a man being in his domain. In other words, that over which he is captain and king. It might include things, places or people.

So what do you have dominion over?

And before you start limiting your answer to that question, think about all of your relationships, about your children, your home and your possessions. Think about your neighbourhood, your career, your children's school and your business. Think about the projects you manage, the teams you coach, and the apprentice you employ. The aim of recognising and acknowledging these things is not to send you on a power trip. Quite the opposite. You are not to be the tyrant, but the servant king of your domain.

Dominion is associated with kingdoms and therefore kings. All of us have these little kingdoms, however humble, unimportant or insignificant we might feel. Your domain might be your shed or merely your toolbox. Something or somewhere which everyone knows they aren't to interfere with because it's yours.

James has a coffee machine at home which no one else is allowed to touch for the simple reason that no one else uses it. He stocks it, cleans it, polishes it and maintains it. It's bundled in there with the lawnmower and his nasal tweezers as being part of his own personal stuff.

Once we start to recognise that all of this is my responsibility, then one of the ways of fathering well is to begin to hand over that domain of responsibility to our children one piece at a time.

Think about it like this. Fatherhood is a lot like flying a kite. The objective is to fly the kite higher and higher. So as you fly, you let out more and more of the string. At first when the string is short, your tweaks have a significant impact. But when the string grows longer eventually it's so long that your tweaks take a long while to have any visible impact. The father's objective is to hand over more and more responsibility. And of course this can start at a very young age.

To the child of seven or eight who wants to have a rabbit for their birthday, by all means get one. But be sure to tell them, 'If you want a rabbit, then this is *your* rabbit. No one else's. How are you going to look after it? I'm here to help you if you need, but you're going to feed it. You're going to clean its hutch.' Or, 'This is your room. Here are the clean sheets. Make the bed. We're here if you need any help.' Or, 'Sure you can have a bike. Here's the bike. Here's a bike lock. This is how it works. If it gets nicked, then you don't have a bike anymore, and you'll have to pay for the next one yourself.'

James' sons are quarter-Japanese. When each of them turns eighteen, he is going to buy them a bonsai tree. This represents something symbolic from their culture, but it also represents something they must take responsibility for, something they must nurture. And if they don't, the tree will die. But if they do and they do it well, then they will be tending to something that might live for a hundred years.

The lessons of this sort of thing for any young Padawan are invaluable. Such wisdom and skills will never grow old.

When James' eldest son, Samson, was one year old, a friend gave James a gold watch to wear for him until he was old enough to wear it for himself. In a way, this symbolises everything that we are trying to say here. The watch itself is precious. It needs looking after. But the time will come when Samson will be ready to take on the responsibility of looking after that watch for himself, and so James will hand it over. The watch then becomes Samson's responsibility until maybe he has a son or a daughter to whom he will one day pass it on.

So what we are saying is, ask yourself the question: What can you pass on to your children now? Whatever age they are, you don't have to wait till they reach some arbitrary marker, their 18th or 21st birthday. It may be something small. It may be some activity they can do for themselves. It may be a physical object to look after. You have to be the judge of when the time is right. And handing over some responsibility to your Padawan does not mean you abdicate all oversight. But the point is, you can start increasing their dominion now.

We want them to flourish. We want them to be free.

To step out as the hero of their own adventure, to stretch the limits of what is possible. To realise their dreams. To slay their dragons. To win their rewards.

And then to return to us, wiser, stronger and ready to share all that they have learned back into their world and with the generations to come.

Conclusion

In some ways it seems pointless trying to conclude a book like this with some sort of pithy comment or illustration, because the realities we've been discussing will go on forever and don't have a fixed end.

As we hope has been clear throughout the book, it's your own individual story, your own individual journey that you need to cultivate. Your success will be defined by what you believe and who you are, and how you bring forth the best of that.

We hope that as you journey towards becoming the Authentic Man that what you take away from this book is the embedding of the ideas in its pages. And that this will allow you to work them out in the right way in your life, in your community and in your world.

Having said that, there are two things we want to reiterate by way of a final sign-off. These are **balance** and **responsibility**. The essence of everything we've discussed boils down to these two concepts.

You need to take responsibility for who you are, for what you've done, for your impact on the world already. And then you need to find balance going forward. By doing that, you are taking responsibility for who you will end up becoming.

Responsibility for your past.

Balance in your present.

Responsibility for your future.

Fine. But what does this look like?

*

There's a famous story from antiquity which the classical poet Homer relates in his epic poem, *The Odyssey*. After the fall of Troy, the Greek hero Odysseus, having incurred the anger of the sea god, Poseidon, is doomed to wander the seas for another ten years before he is able to return home to his wife and family. At a certain point, he is forewarned by the witch Circe that his ship must pass an island inhabited by some mystical creatures called Sirens, whose singing is so beautiful that, upon hearing it, passing sailors steer their ship closer in to shore and so are lured onto the jagged rocks that surround the island and shipwrecked. Those who survive will die on the island, trapped in the thrall of the Sirens' enchanting song. Circe tells Odysseus that if he and his men are to have any chance of escaping this beautiful death-trap, he must block up the ears of his crew. However, she says, if he wants to he could hear the Sirens' song for himself and still live, provided that he orders his crew to first tie him to the mast. Otherwise, upon hearing the song, he will want to throw himself into the sea just to get closer to the alluring Sirens, and so drown. The more he raves at his men to let him go, the tighter they must bind him, Circe says. That way, the ship will pass by the island safely, and Odysseus will be the only man to have heard the wondrous song of the Sirens and survive.

We think Odysseus has something of the Authentic Man about him. He has the passion and self-belief that he can go places that no other man has been, do things no other man has done.

Intrigued by the idea of music so beautiful that it drives men to madness, he decides to hear it for himself and so follows Circe's instructions to the letter. He blocks up his crew's ears with wax and has them lash him to the mast. As they pass the island, Odysseus spies the beautiful Sirens sitting on a meadow by the shore and soon he hears their song. At once, he becomes crazed with the desire to reach the island. But being bound to the mast, all he can do is rave and curse at his crew to let him go. But the more he begs to be cut free, the more ropes they throw around him to bind him all the tighter. At last, the ship passes out of earshot of the Sirens' music, and Odysseus has escaped the beautiful but deadly trap, the only man who ever did so and lived to tell the tale.

This story is multi-faceted; it has so much to it. But the essence of it, which is so powerful, is that Odysseus knew that if he was to overcome a challenge which no one had ever achieved before, he needed literally to bind himself to his responsibility. He needed to ask the men around him to tie him to the very thing that he was already committed to – namely his ship, his crew, his mission to reach home and his commitments that were waiting for him there.

So what does that look like in your life?

We hope this book has outlined many different things for you to think about. But even as you seek ways to apply them in your life, we ask you to do more than that. We ask that you tie yourself into them. So that when the going gets tough, when it looks like you want to stray, you have already forewarned your friends and companions to bind you in even tighter.

What we especially like about this story is that Odysseus didn't avoid entirely hearing the Sirens' music.

There may be some things you feel you can flirt with, stray close to. Often we think that the best way of resisting certain lures in life is to absolutely and totally avoid them. But sometimes those lures cannot be avoided. Or else the thing itself is not inherently wrong or dangerous, and it's only when it is taken or done to excess that it becomes destructive. In this sense, temptation is not something to fear, but something to overcome. As it was for Odysseus, for us resisting temptation is to walk the fine line between hearing the beauty, but not succumbing to it.

This is the point of balance.

Odysseus wanted to do something bold and fraught with risk, which some might think was unwise. But because he did it with enough balance – coupled with his sense of responsibility to his own mission and the men around him – he was able to overcome and to survive.

The story of Odysseus is a story for each of us.

You'll remember that we opened this book with Myles' story about his grandfather. About how crushed Myles was to discover that his grandfather was not the man he had always imagined him to be.

On the one hand, we are all flawed human beings, sufferers of our own weaknesses and foolish mistakes, and so Myles shouldn't judge his grandfather too harshly. But on the other, knowing this doesn't mean Myles has to give in to his own flaws. Nor do you. He can live out a different story if he chooses. So can you.

And that *is* what he chooses.

He wants to imagine that, when his life reaches its end in 20 or 30 or 50 years' time, his own grandchildren will be able to see in him a man to look up to, a man of integrity. That they will not discover some secret double life that undermines the life he presents to his family and the wider world. But rather, here was a man who was the same all the way through. A man on a journey towards becoming the Authentic Man. A journey that starts today.

*

Who do you want to be? What legacy do you want to build?

Your journey starts today.

So take responsibility. Find balance.

And fight and strive to become the Authentic Man.

Appendix A

At many points in this book we have mentioned the Xtreme Character Challenge. By now you will know that James and Myles set this initiative up in the UK, but it is actually running in various forms worldwide. Each country has a different feel, but essentially all are heading in the same direction. Here's a bit more information. But not too much...as a core principle of the experience is ADVENTURE and the definition of an adventure is an activity with an uncertain outcome.

What Is An Xtreme Character Challenge?
An XCC is a mind, body and soul adventure – an active and challenging endurance event for men, out in the wild. The XCC is set up like one endless day; for 72 hours men are confronted with significant physical challenges, deep camaraderie and profound moments of spiritual input. Through the XCC process men find perspective. They evaluate who they are and they find a purpose worth living for.

Who's It For?
The XCC is for all blokes, and if you've read this book it is certainly for you. It is physically tough....but not too tough. You need to come with an open mind and be ready to be challenged. If you are up for it, you can sign up as an individual or with a group.

How Do I sign Up?
Check out: **www.xtremecharacterchallenge.com**

Appendix B

Addiction in any of its many forms is a serious condition to contend with. And while we do not hold ourselves out as experts in any particular field of addiction, we have had experience speaking to many men over the years who have struggled with addiction and seen their lives painfully impacted by its effects. Some of these men have overcome it and found their way to freedom. There are others for whom their struggle continues.

If you feel there is some influence in your life that has a greater hold over you than you would like or which is having a destructive impact on your life, on your relationships or on your ability to live the life you want to be living, then the first positive step you can take towards freedom is to ask for help.

The causes of addiction are varied between different people. Some people are more physiologically addicted, others more psychologically, and still others more through habit. Whatever the root cause of our addiction, we do best when we're in community in recovery.

The 12 Step Programme in its different forms – covering addiction to alcohol, narcotics, gambling or sex – is a tried and tested methodology which we would strongly recommend to anyone struggling with addiction.

People with addictions often do best in their family environment when the family members themselves are getting support. There are also Al-Anon groups for all of the addictions just mentioned. We recommend that 'allies' of those in addiction – people married to or in family relationship with those who are addicted – should also get their own support through an appropriate addictions community.

Every individual's situation is unique and complex, and it may take time and commitment to find a way through to a solution. But we want to encourage you – as for any journey, if you have good people around you, committed to supporting your physical, spiritual and mental wellbeing, then however hard the road, you can make it through.

Appendix C

In chapter 4, we touched on some pretty big questions – such as is there a God? Was I created for a purpose? Is there an afterlife? Does it matter how I live? Is there more to life than what I can immediately see and touch and taste?

We only brush lightly over these because this book does not feel like the place to delve into them to any great depth. But that doesn't mean we don't think they are really important questions, the answers to which have profound implications for how the Authentic Man should choose to live out his life. In fact, we think the Authentic man actively pursues questions of purpose, truth, faith and meaning.

As Socrates, the Greek philosopher, once said, 'The unexamined life is not worth living.'

But it is always good to find the right forum in which you can 'examine' life and ask questions that don't always have easy cut-and-dried answers but nevertheless allow you to grapple with the deeper truths of life. One brilliant forum we would recommend to those who are interested in exploring answers to these questions is Alpha.

Alpha courses are run all over the country throughout the year. You can find a course running near you here: **www.tryalpha.org**

It would seem inauthentic on our part not to identify ourselves as Christians at some point in a book about being authentic. So here it is. One of the many reasons that we follow Jesus Christ is that we think he is the definitive Authentic Man. The ultimate male. The destination. More than this, he not only embodies the ideal, but is also the guide who then empowers us to reach it. This is especially comforting when we find ourselves wounded or lame or broken on the road, we need a helping hand stronger than ourselves to keep us going.

We think it is significant that the first words Christ utters in the Gospel of John are a question, 'What are you seeking?'

It's a question for every single one of us.
What are *you* seeking?

We believe the clue to finding what we seek lies in his very next words. This time, an invitation.

'Come and you will see.'

Printed in Great Britain
by Amazon